M
TALES

Stories of Minnesota TV, Radio, Publications and Personalities

By Sheri O'Meara and Martin Keller

the *Minnesota* series

Clancy and Willie and their cast of characters were a fixture on WCCO-TV in the '60s and '70s. (photos: courtesy Timothy D. Kehr)

Welcome to Media Tales

M *edia Tales,* the third book in The Minnesota Series, delivers a behind-the-scenes look at Minnesota media. Inside, you'll find stories and rare photos of Minnesota television, radio, magazines, newpapers and advertising. We hope you'll enjoy this look back at the faces and places that comprise Minnesota's rich media history.

Past and coming books in The Minnesota Series include: *Music Legends, Storms!, Storms 2* (our next title), *Political Stars, Sports Legends, Famous Crimes, Newsmakers, Urban Legends* and more. In each edition, you'll find informative and entertaining stories, and rare photographs. Pick up books at retailers across the state or at www.minnesotaseries.com.

Enjoy *Media Tales* and all the books in the series!

Authors **Sheri O'Meara, Martin Keller**
Design and Layout **Phil Tippin**
Proofreader **Marsha Kitchel**
Web Consultant **Risdall Advertising, New Brighton, Minn.**
Printing **Bang Printing, Brainerd, Minn.**
Publishing and Production Management **Jim Bindas, Books & Projects LLC**
Publishers **D Media: Debra Gustafson Decker, Dale Decker**

Dedicated to the Memory of Carol Ratelle Leach

©2007 by D Media Inc., 4601 Excelsior Blvd #301, Minneapolis, Minn. 55416. (952) 926-3950. dmedia@juno.com. www.minnesotaseries.com. Subscriptions available at www.minnesotaseries.com

ISBN 9780978795627

Library of Congress Control Number 2007927905

Contents

Foreword **5**

Chapter 1: **Television** **6**
Making Memories, Seeing Stars

Chapter 2: **Radio** **46**
Minnesota Tunes In

Chapter 3: **Public TV and Radio** **66**
Educating, Entertaining, Coming of Age

Chapter 4: **Magazines** **80**
Land of 10,000 Stories

Chapter 5: **Newspapers** **94**
The Scoop on Papers Past and Present

Chapter 6: **Advertising** **108**
From the Land of Sky Blue Water

On the cover: Roger Awsumb as Casey Jones and Dave Moore (who anchored both WCCO's real news and the spoof "Bedtime Newz"). photos: courtesy Pavek Museum

Foreword

*They may forget what you said, but they will never
forget how you made them feel.*   —Carl Buechner

During my career as a journalist, I've learned the best
communicators understand that the most memorable
stories resound in the heart.

Yes, clearly laying out the facts and untangling
confusing situations is a great skill. But in the end, it's not the
words or images that matter most, but the feelings you
experience. Connecting the heart of the community with the
world's unfolding drama is the work of the best of the best.

This book highlights many of the best in Minnesota's
media history—the storied people and institutions that made
those connections so effectively. Minnesotans are national
leaders, and the media people follow that pattern. Get set to
read about some of this country's most memorable broadcasters and print personalities.

A good journalist listens. *Media Tales* authors looked
back on the people Minnesotans have listened to, watched,
read and been entertained by over the years. Enjoy with me
now the results of that review.

Mike Pomeranz, *Anchor,* KARE-11 TV, *Mpls St. Paul* (ͯ)

In early Minnesota television broadcasts, KSTP beamed Gopher football to Twin Citians with the first TV sets. (photo: courtesy Pavek Museum)

Minnesota's Television Stations

KRWF, KSAX **Alexandria**; KSMN,KWCM **Appleton**;
KAAL **Austin**; KAWE **Bemidji**;
KBJR, KDLH, KQDS, WDIO/WIRT, WDSE **Duluth**;
KEYC **Mankato**; KBBR/KVRR **Moorhead**;
KTTC, KXLT **Rochester**;
WCCO, KMSP, KSTP, KSTC, KARE, KTCA/KTCI, WFTC,
WUCW, KPXM **Twin Cities**

Television
Making Memories, Seeing Stars

In 1933, as Americans huddled around their radios to listen to *The Lone Ranger* begin a 21-year run and to new president Franklin D. Roosevelt promising to pull us out of the Great Depression—Minnesota quietly had its first experimental telecast. On Aug. 4, 1933, W9XAT, a mechanical TV station licensed to Dr. George Young, owner of WDGY-AM, began its short life when a picture of WDGY personality Clellan Card and Minneapolis Mayor William F. Kunze shaking hands was transmitted to a receiver at the Minneapolis courthouse. It was a non-event in its day—likely more for the engineers of WDGY to test the television equipment they designed and built. After sporadic programming (with performers working in the dark, facing a light beamed from the camera), W9XAT gave up after a year. But it was a crystal ball into the future. Card would go on to become a Minnesota television celebrity as Axel, and television would change our lives.

In 1938, as W9XAT's television license expired and mechanical television became obsolete, Stanley E. Hubbard, owner of KSTP radio, was busy planning, buying the first television camera commercially available from RCA. Broadcasting was in its infancy, but Hubbard had already made a name for himself with "firsts" in the industry. Besides launching one of the four first radio stations in the Twin Cities, Hubbard (who was also an aviation pioneer) was part of the first successful communication between planes (1921), had launched the first radio network between Chicago and the Twin Cities (1925) and pioneered the first local broadcast news-gathering bureau (1925), merging his two passions by using aircraft for gathering news from throughout Minnesota. He would go on to create many more firsts in his legendary career.

RCA introduced electronic television to the country at the 1939 World's Fair (with an appearance on air by FDR, which made him the first U.S. president to appear on TV) and began regularly scheduled broadcasting. In 1941, the first commercially produced program was broadcast on the National Broadcasting Co. (NBC).

On April 19, 1947, the Twin City Television Lab opened, designed to train future broadcasters in the new medium. Many trained here would go on to jobs in national broadcasting. Mel Jass played a major role in designing and managing the Lab. Jass started in TV at WCCO—doing everything from anchoring newscasts to hosting *Popeye's Club House*. (Later, after a stint in Hollywood, which included roles in several Alfred Hitchcock films and *Twilight Zone* episodes, Jass would become the best-known television pitchman in the Twin Cities, and one of the most recognized personalities on local television. Many remember him best as host of Channel 11's *Matinee Movie*. Joel and Ethan Coen apparently do—they credit Jass for launching their interest in films.)

By the end of 1947, if you asked kids anywhere in the country what time it was, they would respond: "It's Howdy Doody time!" *Howdy Doody* first aired Dec. 27, 1947, and is credited for selling more people on the future of television than any other single event. Millions of children tuned in to the daily live kids' show. (Good thing they didn't know that Buffalo Bob and Clarabell the clown had issues. Clarabell was fired first in 1950, because "he"—yes, a man in real life— couldn't play an instrument and was too rowdy with his seltzer bottle spraying. Kids apparently demanded the "old" clown back when they saw the replacement, so he returned. Later, Clarabell would be shown the door again when he led other cast members in an uprising over more money. But living well is the best revenge. Clarabell later regrouped and starred in his own show, *Captain Kangaroo*. Offstage, he was Bob Keeshan.)

KSTP-TV went on the air April 27, 1948, officially the first TV station in the Upper Midwest, broadcasting for 12 to 14 hours per week to the 3,000 television sets in the Twin Cities at the time.

On May 8, 1948, the first locally produced children's television show in the Twin Cities aired on KSTP. *Riddle Griddle* was a quiz show for kids that had originated on radio, emceed by announcer Jimmy Valentine.

Channel 4 TV, located in the old Radio City Theater in Minneapolis, went on the air July 1, 1949, with call letters WTCN. With 26 employees, three live cameras and one film camera, WTCN launched just six hours short of a deadline imposed by the Federal Communications Commission.

KSTP-TV debuted the nation's first regularly scheduled nightly 10 p.m. newscast in 1949, with Bill Ingram as anchor. According to the Minnesota Broadcasters Assoc.: "Ingram's skills in reporting, editing, and narrating, and his blend of dignity and warmth helped set trends that were adopted by television stations and news teams throughout the country." Ingram went on to KROC-TV Rochester, then WMAQ-TV

Chicago, and then WDSM-TV Duluth. Viewers loved his sign-off: "That's it ... that's the news. Thanks for your company," accompanied by a wink.

Also in '49, Bud Kraehling entered Minneapolis/St. Paul-area television on Channel 4. In 1950, he began a five-minute 10 p.m. television weather report for Taystee Bread. "I just happened into it," Kraehling said later. "The first time I did weather on TV I was substituting for a man who went on vacation and it was sponsored by Taystee Bread. I did a better commercial, I guess, than he did, so the sponsor had me stay on." Over the years, he wrote forecasts on the Weather Window for crowds gathered outside the studio, and later worked from the Shell Weather Tower. "We started what we called the happy talk, the bridge between news and weather," Kraehling once said of his years with anchor Dave Moore. "He [Moore] said later we set a curse on the entire industry for doing so."

Coaxial cable came to the Twin Cities in 1950, enabling network programming to begin and allowing Twin Cities television stations to carry most new programs on a direct "live" basis.

By 1951, Mel Jass was hosting *Show People* on Channel 4. Later would come his *Mel Jass Show,* then *Mel's Almanac,* a new *Mel Jass Show* and *Matinee Movie.*

Now the alphabet soup started. In 1952 Channel 4's WTCN-TV merged with WCCO Radio, and was given the call sign WCCO-TV. During its first week of operation, WCCO-TV presented about 35 hours of programming.

In 1953, a new WTCN started broadcasting on Channel 11 with a time-sharing agreement with station WMIN.

Each station would use the transmitter for two hours, then allow the other channel to take over for the next two. The two stations eventually merged. The original transmitter for WTCN and WMIN was located atop the Foshay Tower in Minneapolis, the tallest building in the city at the time. A growing city meant that the transmitter would eventually have to go, and it was moved to Shoreview in 1972. Additionally, the new transmitter greatly increased the station's reception area.

Stuart A. Lindman signed WMIN on the air on Channel 11 for the first time in 1953, serving as newscaster, news director and program director. After the station merged with WTCN in 1956, he continued as radio news director and anchor until 1973, when he became director of public affairs. When the station changed its call letters to WUSA and later to KARE, it was Stuart A. Lindman who was the first to sign them on.

In 1953 Sherm Booen created *World of Aviation*, a program he produced and hosted on WCCO. The popular show ran for 28 years, the world's only regularly scheduled aviation television program, until his retirement in 1982.

In Austin, KAAL went on air Aug. 17, 1953 as KMMT. It is the longest-tenured ABC affiliate in the Upper Midwest. The same year in Rochester, KROC (now KTTC) signed on as the first television station in that town.

In 1954, Helen and Richard Brown's American Institute of the Air school they started in 1946 in Minneapolis was renamed Brown Institute, when courses in electronics, computer programming and television production were added.

Now we were in the middle of The Golden Age of Television, when television became a popular mass medium.

TV stations did not broadcast 24 hours per day—limitations in the design of transmitters resulted in a 12-hour to 18-hour-per-day schedule. Radio continued to play a role. Even *I Love Lucy* drew heavily from radio as many of those scripts were rewrites from Lucille Ball's late-1940s radio show *My Favorite Husband.* Shows like *Our Miss Brooks, The Burns and Allen Show* and *The Jack Benny Show* ran on both radio and TV. We started tuning in: *Father Knows Best, Honeymooners, Leave it to Beaver, The Lone Ranger, The Three Stooges.*

By the early-'50s, children's programming was big business. Back then, daytime belonged to the children, as kids discovered the magic box that became a fixture in their homes and their lives. Moms allowed big, unsightly "rabbit ears" to appear in their formal living rooms. A new era began. In Minnesota, there were some key early players:

In 1953, Daryl Laub created and starred in *Skipper Daryl* on Channel 11. Later that year he added a tattered clown called J. P. Patches to the roster. (J. P. Patches, along with Oregon's Rusty Nails, is considered to be one of Matt Groening's influences in creating *The Simpsons* character Krusty the Clown.) Eventually Laub would make the move to KSTP, change his clown to T. N. Tatters and promote his nautical character to *Captain Daryl.* After his stint on television, Laub would go on to work in KSTP's radio division, spending nearly 30 years at what is now KQRS, eventually becoming station manager.

In 1954, WCCO-TV needed a strong entry in children's programming. So they tapped one of their biggest stars on WCCO Radio—Clellan Card (who was also the star of the 1933 experimental telecast on W9XAT). By the end of the '30s Card was the most popular personality on one of the biggest radio stations in the country. His "Doughnut Dunking Jamborees" (held each April Fool's Day) regularly drew crowds of more than 2,000 people to watch a radio broadcast at 7 a.m. His recitation of a Scandihoovian lampoon of "The Night Before Christmas" was a beloved annual tradition from 1938 to 1965.

Card was recruited to play a variation of his wacky Scandinavian character, Axel. The new kids' program featured Card as Axel plus Old Log Theater founder/director Don Stolz playing Axel's silent dog, Towser. Soon, a cat character named Tallulah, also played by Don Stolz, was added to the cast. Later, Mary Davies as Carmen the Nurse joined the company, and by the end, she became Axel's co-host.

According to Stolz, the first program was nearly the last. Like most television programs of the time, it was broadcast live. There was no script. According to Julian West's *What a Card! The Story of Clellan Card and "Axel and His Dog"*:

WCCO-TV had been running promotional announcements for the program during the summer, inviting kids to send in jokes for Axel to read on the air. So he did. Plucking a letter from the pile, he read aloud: "Why does the chicken cross the road?" Perhaps chuckling at the notion that the first joke on his new program would be the world's oldest chestnut, Axel read the punch line before he realized what he was saying: "Because she's laying the farmer on the other side!" Miraculously, the show wasn't immediately cancelled.

Although Axel was apt to ad-lib anything at any time, the Saturday morning version of *Axel and His Dog* was especially wild, according to Stoltz in West's book: "This was all live, you have to remember that," Stolz noted. "Clellan was a night person, and I certainly was, operating a theater, and half of the floormen were night people, and I'll tell you, anything could happen on that show at that hour of the morning."

Axel was a huge success. There were times when more than 25 percent of all Twin Cities televisions were tuned in. In October 1954, *Axel and His Dog* was the first local television colorcast in the Twin Cities.

Also in 1954, another beloved Minnesota children's TV character appeared on WTCN-TV for the first time: engineer Casey Jones, played by Roger Awsumb. Thousands of kids went home from school for *Lunch with Casey* every day. For 19 years kids spent one of the best parts of their day with Casey and former Ice Capades skater Lynn Dwyer (aka Roundhouse Rodney). Each day kids would watch for their names on Birthday Train, and Casey would have lunch delivered by a local restaurant. Guests like the animal handler from the Como Park Zoo, or a musical act would sometimes entertain. Occasionally Casey and Roundhouse produced musical segments, usually lip-synching to goofy songs (like the Christmas-time classic "Walking in My Winter Underwear" and the ever-popular "I Love Onions").

Beginning in the mid-'50s, you could find kids at play staring into a "magic mirror" and intoning, "Romper stomper bomper boo" or chanting, "Do be a do bee, don't be a don't be." Yes, Romper Room had arrived, in standard syndication and also sold like a franchise with a different local host in each city. It would enjoy a long run.

During this time, WTCN-TV also featured *Wrangler Steve*, a cowboy played by Steve Cannon (later of WCCO radio fame), and *Captain 11*, a uniformed space ranger originally played by Jim Lange (later host of the national game show *The Dating Game*).

The fun and games of the local kids' shows masked grownup ratings battles. In the Julian West book, the promotion director of WCCO-TV, Gene Godt, recalls that the late-afternoon time period—the slot for most local children's programs during the '50s— was "... the most intensely competitive 90 minutes of television produced locally in our five-station market." He also noted that children were "...one of the most important audiences, for the kids not only directly influence their parents' choice of products, but to a large extent determine which is the favorite channel on their family television set."

"We were beating the other stations that were running news and weather and sports at that time," Steve Cannon (aka Wrangler Steve) remembers. "Shows you who was controlling the dial back in 1953 and '54. It was the children."

Other local kids' programs included *The Popeye and Pete Show; Captain Ken* played by Ken Wagner, who did his show from a riverboat set before the character "retired" and became *Grandpa Ken*; and *The Happy Hour with Fred & Friends*.

Television stations continued cropping up in Minnesota. In Duluth: WDSM was the first television station in town, signing on days before NBC's KDAL-TV (now KDLH).

In 1955, KMSP began broadcasting as KEYD on March 12. One of its first news reporters was Harry Reasoner, who would go on to national fame on *60 Minutes*. The station became independent until 1961.

At the end of April 1955, WTCN and WMIN, which had been sharing a frequency, merged under new ownership as WTCN. WTCN was an affiliate of ABC. Also that year, KSTP began broadcasting NBC network programs in color.

Meanwhile news divisions were staffing up. Pilot Ralph Dolan began flying for Hubbard Broadcasting in 1956, and in 1957 he became the first television news pilot in Minnesota, flying KSTP TV's "News Hawk" plane. (Later at Hubbard, he would become operations manager and go on to found local programs including *Good Company*, and later still, became station manager.)

In 1957, WCCO sought a new anchor for its 10 p.m. newscast, and a young Dave Moore got the job when Walter Cronkite turned it down. Moore had little background in journalism, but we loved him—lapping up his *Bedtime Newz* late-night satire, *Moore on Sunday* and *The Moore Report*. Moore (who also taught drama classes and was active in community theater) would go on to anchor the 10 p.m. news until 1985, the 6 p.m. news until 1991 and *Moore on Sunday* until he became ill in 1997 and died in 1998. It was no surprise when a poll taken in the 1980s, we learned that the best-known face in Minnesota belonged to Dave Moore.

In 1958, KMGM was renamed KMSP, and a live event featuring Axel at Excelsior Amusement Park at Lake Minnetonka drew 12,000 people.

Channel 4 added more to its kids' lineup in 1959 with *Commodore Cappy*, starring John Gallos. The show morphed into *Clancy the Keystone Cop*, and by 1963, it was *Clancy the Cop*, then *Clancy and Company*. Clancy had a sidekick detective, Willie Ketchum (Allan Lotsberg). The new show, set in a small detective agency, added Carmen the Nurse (from Axel's show), and ran weekday mornings on WCCO.

In January 1959, Axel's rating was nearly three times that of the nearest competitor, *American Bandstand.* Soupy Sales also debuted on TV in 1959. Kids and adults alike watched him on Channel 11 on Saturdays at noon.

Bill Carlson started on WCCO in 1959, working in several roles over the years including news anchor. In Mankato, KEYC signed on Oct. 5, 1960, just in time to broadcast the first game of the World Series that night.

On April 18, 1961, KMSP became the area's ABC affiliate, an arrangement that would last until 1979. KSTP became the country's first all-color station. WTCN lost the ABC affiliation to KMSP and became independent. KMSP would feature the wildly popular All-Star Wrestling, starring Verne Gagne. Gagne's promotional group, the AWA, dominated wrestling in the Midwest.

In 1962, during the first international live broadcast via the new Telstar satellite, WCCO-TV's mobile units provided the feed for three networks, for a special program from the Black Hills showing Mount Rushmore to the world.

The 1960s also brought professional baseball to Minnesota. For years, fans watched the Twins on WTCN, with play-by-play from Halsey Hall.

In 1964, a local rock 'n' roll show, *A Date With Dino,* was broadcast on Channel 9. A teenage Nancy Nelson (who later would become a product spokesperson and marry broadcaster Bill Carlson) was in the cast.

By the early-1960s, about 80 percent of American households had a television set. At that point, sitcoms and dramas dropped out of radio and became the domain of TV. Television entered adolescence in the '60s, but the medium was still young, and we treated it differently then than we do today. Back then, watching television was an activity you scheduled. Families everywhere gathered to watch *Andy Griffith, Dick Van Dyke* and *Dobie Gillis*. And later, *Batman, Hogan's Heroes, The Monkees* and *Star Trek*.

In November 1966, WCCO went to all color. In January 1967, KMSP went to all color. Clellan Card continued to play Axel until just weeks before his death on April 13, 1966.

While the world was changing quickly in the '60s, news stories were still shot and edited on film. Former Channel 11 photographer Doug Froemming said of the cameras, "You've got about 20 seconds of wind, and then it runs out. Then you have to rewind it, so you had to make sure when you were shooting you didn't start too soon. Or it would stop right in the middle of an important shot."

Carl "Cully" Bloomquist founded the Iron Range's first television station, WIRT-TV Hibbing, in 1967, and later helped develop cable television systems in Grand Forks and in Virginia. He also owned radio station WEVE Eveleth, which he operated for more than 30 years.

While still in high school, Mark Rosen joined WCCO-TV in 1969 as part-time sports writer/reporter. He'd go on to become sports director, anchor and reporter.

In 1970 at KSTP, Stan Turner came aboard as main anchor. Shortly afterward came Marcia Fluer, first as an entertainment reporter, then as a political correspondent, general assignment reporter and weekend anchor. She was one of the first female television anchors in the Twin Cities.

In 1970, WTCN went to all color.

And then came Mary:

Beginning in 1970, Minnesotans and the rest of the country tuned in each week to watch Mary Richards toss up her hat on Nicollet Mall, in the opening scene of *Mary Tyler Moore*, a show about a fictitious TV newsroom in Minneapolis. (A real passerby, an older woman, was caught on camera in the background of the opening scene, puzzled by the shenanigans in the street. She was Hazel Frederick, a Minnesota resident who happened to be out shopping that day.) *Entertainment Weekly* would later rank this scene No. 2 on their list of The 100 Greatest Moments In Television. When the Minnesota Vikings played three Super Bowls in the '70s, the opening montage included a scene with Mary washing her car while wearing the No. 10 home jersey of quarterback Fran Tarkenton.

By the early-1970s, the glory days of local children's programming were ending. Fewer kids were coming home for lunch, and Action for Children's Television now prevented hosts from doing commercials. The last *Lunch With Casey* aired on Dec. 29, 1972. It was an auspicious farewell. Minnesota Twins legend Harmon Killebrew stopped by to say goodbye, and Minneapolis Mayor Charles Stenvig put in a surprise appearance.

But with Casey gone, we still rushed home to see national shows *Gilligan's Island, Bewitched, Happy Days, The Brady Bunch, Green Acres, The Beverly Hillbillies, Petticoat Junction* and *The Partridge Family*.

In 1974, Ron Magers joined KSTP, where he would reign as anchor until 1981. While there, he was obviously an influence on little brother Paul, who originally planned to be a lawyer. But before long, Paul Magers was working behind the scenes at KSTP as a technician, dispatcher and producer. He would not stay off camera for long.

But what if you missed a show or didn't like what was on? Wouldn't it be nice to put in a movie of your own? Enter the VCR, and the format wars. First there was Betamax, a home VCR was introduced by Sony in 1975. VHS was introduced by JVC the following year. VHS won, but it was a long ordeal. The two battled for sales in what has become known as the original and definitive format war.

In the mid-'70s, David Letterman almost became the weatherman at Channel 9. According to an article by Jeff R. Lonto: Letterman, who worked as a weatherman in Indianapolis in the mid-'70s, has mentioned in interviews that he came close to moving to the Twin Cities. He told the *Minneapolis Star Tribune* that he was offered the job with Channel 9 and almost took it, even though the pay was no better than what he was getting in Indianapolis. But on his way back to the airport, "I saw these big fences down the median of the highway. I asked the driver what they were, and he said it was for the snow. I decided then that I'm not doing that. It just wasn't worth it to be that uncomfortable for the same amount of money."

Barry ZeVan the Weatherman and his peek-a-boo reports would have been Letterman's competition over at Channel 5. *Star Tribune* related that ZeVan interviewed Letterman years later, and that Letterman said, "You know, you're really responsible for where I am. I came up to audition to do the weather on Channel 9, on KMSP...I watched you the first night and I didn't want to compete with you."

At Channel 4, the kids' shows lasted longer but the end finally came when the station announced the cancellation of its long-running children's programs to make way for *Donahue*. On March 25, 1977, Clancy, Willie and Carmen made their exit, with Clancy reciting an Irish blessing as his parting words.

Don Shelby joined WCCO-TV as a news anchor in 1978. He was soon paired with Pat Miles as the anchor of the weekend news. Later, Miles became Paul Magers' co-anchor on the early-evening news programs on KARE.

1979 was a confusing year for viewers. KSTP became an ABC affiliate, WTCN became an NBC affiliate, and KMSP went independent.

On late-night TV, stations across the state signed off at midnight with the American flag and the national anthem. (In the Twin Cities, this happened only after Pastor Reuben Youngdahl of Mount Olivet Lutheran Church gave the benediction on WCCO.) In the late-'70s, Timothy D. Kehr could be seen across the dial overnight in the metro area with programs featuring serials, movies and reruns. Kehr combined insights, guests, nostalgia, promotion and a gift for the bizarre in shows that would go on to span two decades and six stations. With the dawn of cable and onset of 24-hour programming, late-night shows like Kehr's vanished.

Cable television was now a reality, and Stanley S. (son of Stanley E.) Hubbard pioneered a satellite television network in 1981.

Elsewhere in the Hubbard empire: From 1982 to 1994, when nationally syndicated talk shows ruled the daytime airwaves, KSTP ran a talk program of its own—*Good Company*.

It would become the No. 1 rated locally produced program in the nation, co-hosted by married couple Sharon Anderson and Steve Edelman. The show included a cast of regulars, among them—Gary Lumpkin (the game-for-anything field host), bargain-hunter Vicki Audette and Corbin Seitz (now co-host on KARE's weekday *Showcase Minnesota,* along with Rob Hudson). Edelman would go on to run Edelman Productions, a company that produces TV shows for Food Network, HGTV, The History Channel and DIY, with Anderson hosting a few of them. KARE-11 weekend anchor Joan Steffend would also go on to enjoy a long run as host of Edelman's *Decorating Cents* on HGTV.

Two new independents began UHF broadcasting. WFBT signed on Sept. 13, 1982. The call letters stood for W Family Bible Television. The station was on Channel 29 and featured a morning show, *Breakfast With Casey.* The station was sold in 1984 and changed to KITN. In 1988 it became the local Fox affiliate and changed the call letters to WFTC (We're Fox Twin Cities). In 2002, WFTC became a UPN station and became UPN29.

In 1983, Gannett Broadcasting bought WTCN, and Diana Pierce and Ron's little brother, Paul, started as anchors. Paul Magers' 20-year reign ended in his leaving the market in 2003. Upon leaving KARE, he said the story that affected him most while in Minnesota was the abduction of Jacob Wetterling in 1989. Diana remains at the anchor desk, focusing on family and lifestyle topics.

In 1984, Doug Kruhoeffer started work as Paul Douglas, meteorologist on Channel 11. He launched "backyard" weather, reporting from outside the studio. Minnesotans tuned in to watch him brave the elements.

Also 1984, KSTP was the first in the country to include live satellite-fed news reports in local news broadcasts.

And we were watching *Laverne & Shirley, One Day at a Time, Welcome Back Kotter, Barretta, Starsky & Hutch, Hillstreet Blues, Mork & Mindy, Cagney & Lacy*. Our Saturday mornings were for *Fat Albert and the Gang, Scooby Doo* and *The Jetsons*.

On July 4, 1985, WTCN became WUSA. In 1986, KMSP became the local affiliate for the new Fox network, but lost it in 1988. WUSA became KARE.

KARE made weather history on July 18, 1986 when helicopter pilot Max Messmer and photojournalist Tom Empey filmed a tornado in the air. KARE broadcast images of the funnel for 30 minutes. In the years to come, this first aerial video of a tornado was heavily studied by meteorologists, and contributed significantly to what is known about tornado formation.

In 1988, Fox affiliation moved from KMSP to KITN, and KMSP became independent. Robyne Robinson would reign at KMSP, becoming the first African-American to anchor a local prime-time newscast, and the first black woman appointed senior anchor at a Twin Cities news organization. She would be paired with Jeff Passolt, who started media life covering sports for Channel 11.

By the late-1980s, 98 percent of all homes in the country had at least one TV set. On average, Americans watched four hours of television per day. An estimated two-thirds of Americans got most of their news about the world from TV, and nearly half got all of their news from TV.

Rick Kupchella started at KARE 11 in 1989.

In 1994 KITN became WFTC on October 1. In January 1995, KLGT became affiliated with Warner Brothers, and KMSP became affiliated with United Paramount.

The Late Show with David Letterman did a Minneapolis-themed show on May 9, 1997. On WCCO, anchors Don Shelby and Amelia Santaniello performed a scripted "breaking news" bit, in which Shelby declared that he had a gopher in his pants named Carlos. Kirby Puckett also guest-starred.

In the late-1990s and early-2000s, DVD gradually overtook VHS as the most popular format for playback of prerecorded video. KMSP became a Fox affiliate. KBJR in Duluth was destroyed by a 1997 fire: The station's newsroom and offices moved to WDSE almost immediately to continue broadcasting, and later rebuilt. Dennis Douda, an anchor and reporter for WCCO-TV, joined the staff in 1998.

Frank Vascellaro debuted with his wife, Amelia Santaniello, on WCCO at 6 on Thursday, June 29, 2006. They are the first married couple to co-anchor a daily news program in the Twin Cities. Prior to joining WCCO, Vascellaro worked at KARE anchoring the 5, 6 and 10 p.m. news. Meanwhile, at KARE-11, Mike Pomerantz (a former pro baseball player whose career included a stint in the Minnesota Twins minor-league system) took over anchor duties, paired with Julie Nelson, with Randy Shaver on sports.

Also in 2006, KSTP started the only 4 p.m. newscast in the market, going up against WCCO's airing of *The Oprah Winfrey Show*.

By this time, Minneapolis-St. Paul ranked 13th or 14th largest television market, depending on the source, and it's clear television had grown up. Trained broadcasters and new technology had changed the way Minnesotans see the world. Cable and satellite TV had changed viewing patterns and expectations, and the internet and HDTV are changing them further. But in other ways, our Minnesota roots are still showing. Bud Kraehling's Shell Weather Tower and the Weather Window may have no place in modern TV weathercasts. But Belinda Jensen, Sven Sundgaard and the team still trudge out to the KARE-11 backyard every day to give the weather reports, just as Paul Douglas did in the '80s (and still does, albeit from the rooftop of WCCO-TV).

Callsign W9XAT—issued to that first television station in Minnesota back in 1933—was left unused until recently when it was granted to the Twin City Experimental Amateur Television Society.

Players from the golden days of television may be long gone from Minnesota TV programming, but they live on in other ways. Don Stolz wrote a play called *Axel and His Dog* based on his own experiences playing Axel's animal sidekicks on the TV show. The play has run at Great American History Theater and Stolz's Old Log Theater. "Willie Ketchum" (aka Allan Lotsberg) helped launch a local cable children's show *Captain McCool* and he runs a senior theater company called New Fogie Follies.

Nostalgic fans can now find Casey, Axel and dozens of other old TV friends in photos, film clips and audio all over the Internet. It's fitting. Everything old is new again, and well-loved characters from the early days of Minnesota television have a new life in cyberspace. 📡

WCCO TELEVISION
MINNEAPOLIS, MINNESOTA

4:55
TO
5:00 PM
WEEKDAYS

ROCKO DYNE
with COLONEL BLEEP

This five-minute program pulls more mail each week than any other Channel 4 show day-after-day.

ROCKO DYNE is portrayed by Channel 4's veteran performer, Jack Hastings. He appears on the program dressed as a spaceman, who lives on Satellite Four.

Youngsters are invited to send postcards with their name, address, age and phone number. These are placed in the "Rocket Barrel."

Before Colonel Bleep's animated film question is run with its multiple choice answers, ROCKO DYNE draws a card and places a call to a lucky youngster. A correct answer gives the winner a choice of the prizes on the set and a chance at a big prize.

ROCKO DYNE with Colonel Bleep offers ideal merchandising opportunities to sponsors through proof of purchase, sampling, and prizes. ROCKO DYNE is also available for personal appearances on behalf of his sponsor's product in the Twin City Area.

WCCO-TELEVISION
CHANNEL 4

PETERS, GRIFFIN & WOODWARD, INC.
NATIONAL REPS.

2-59

Spaceman Rocko Dyne was an early entry in children's entertainment in the '50s.
(courtesy Timothy D.Kehr)

Pinky Lee started in Minnesota and achieved fame nationally on NBC.
(photo: courtesy Timothy D. Kehr)

Clockwise from top left, JP Patches, Joe The Cook, Commodore Cappy and *Romper Room* were early entrants in children's shows across the dial.
(photos: courtesy Timothy D. Kehr and Pavek Museum)

Popeye's Clubhouse and Casey and Roundhouse entertained children for generations in the Twin Cities. (photos: courtesy KARE 11 and Timothy D. Kehr)

Clellan Card as Axel and Mary Davies as Carmen the Nurse entertained children (and adults with a wink) from *Axel's Treehouse* on WCCO TV in the Twin Cities. (photos: courtesy Timothy D. Kehr)

Pastor Reuben Youngdahl of Mt. Olivet in Minneapolis closed the broadcast day on *Live for Today* before the flag and national anthem on WCCO.

WCCO studios in the '50s. Look closely and find a young Dave Moore and other personalities. (photo: courtesy Pavek Museum)

KDAL TV and Radio, later KDLH-TV had bright, new studios in Duluth in the 1960s.
(photo: courtesy Pavek Museum)

WTCN was on the scene to broadcast early games at Met Stadium.
(photo: courtesy Pavek Museum)

Jim Hutton hosted entertainment shows mostly on KSTP. (photo: courtesy Timothy D. Kehr)

Sunset Valley Barn Dance was a kind of early *Prairie Home Companion* on KSTP in
Minneapolis and St. Paul. (photo: courtesy Timothy D. Kehr)

Timothy D. Kehr was seen on late-night TV across the dial in the Twin Cities for over two decades with live studio antics and movie serial insights.

Nancy Nelson hosted *What's New?* on WTCN for many years. Here with Cesar Romero, Nelson is married to WCCO's Bill Carlson and is famous for her national infomercials. (photo: courtesy KARE 11)

Clockwise from top left, Arley Haberly, Jimmy Valentine, Dick Enroth and Frank Buetel informed and entertained Minnesotans across the dial. Enroth broadcast the Minneapolis Lakers, Buetel the Twins and Minnesota Fighting Saints hockey. (photo: courtesy Timothy D. Kehr and Pavek Museum)

WTCN·TV
Metromedia
Minneapolis - St. Paul
11

Mel Jass hosted entertainment and variety shows on both TV and radio. He is probably best remembered for his movie call-in show on WTCN in the Twin Cities and when asking wives what their husband does for work, responding: "Well he's got a good job!" (photo: courtesy Pavek Museum)

Hank Meadows was the resident chef on WTCN in the '60s and '70s, here pictured with Casey and Roundhouse. (photo: courtesy KARE-11)

All Star Wrestling, featuring Wally Karbo, The Crusher, Verne Gagne and others, was filmed first in the WTCN studios at the Calhoun Beach Club in Minneapolis and later here at new studios in Golden Valley. (photo courtesy Al DeRusha)

Clockwise from top left, anchor Bill Ingram; Tony Parker, sports; Dean Montgomery, anchor; and WCCO weather icon Bud Kraehling covered the news for stations in the Twin Cities and across Minnesota. (photos: courtesy Pavek Museum)

Clockwise from top left, John MacDougall, Bob Ryan, Johnny Morris and Al Tighe, combined to form the KSTP news team in the 1960s. (photos courtesy Pavek Museum)

TV pioneer Stuart A. Lindman anchored news and weather reports for Channel 11 in the Twin Cities. (photo: courtesy Pavek Museum)

The Scene Tonight featuring Hal Scott, George Rice, Skip Loescher, Dave Moore and Bud Kraehling launched WCCO into the modern era of "anchor desk" news in the early-'70s. (photo: courtesy Pavek Museum)

Ron Magers, left, with ABC 7 Chicago, led KSTP in Minneapolis/St. Paul to the top of the ratings in the '70s and '80s. His brother Paul followed him as a ratings leader at KARE. Barry ZeVan, right, brought humor and a peek-a-boo style to Twin Cities weather on KSTP and later KARE. (photos: courtesy ABC 7 Chicago, Barry ZeVan, Pavek Museum)

The KSTP news team of the '80s featured Ed Karow, Dave Dahl, Jason Davis, Caroline Brookter, Neil Murray, Dr. Michael Breen, Dennis Feltgen, Cyndy Brucato, Stan Turner, Bob Bruce, Arthur Ballet, Marcia Fleur and Robb Leer. KSTP's ratings were a dominant 50 percent audience share during the '70s and '80s in the Twin Cities.

Clockwise from top left: Joan Steffend, Jeff Passolt, Rod Grams and Ralph Jon Fritz are lasting as Minnesota personalities. Steffend moved from KARE to her own show on HGTV. Passolt moved from KARE sports to anchor KMSP News, Grams from Channel 9 to the U.S. Senate. Ralph Jon Fritz has covered sports on WCCO for decades in the Twin Cities. (photos: courtesy KARE 11 and Pavek Museum)

Duluth television legend Dennis Anderson is flanked here by Steve LePage and Ken Chapin from the 1990s WDIO/WIRT Eyewitness News Team. (photo: courtesy WDIO/WIRT)

Jason Davis' *On The Road* segments and specials have informed and entertained Minnesotans for decades on KSTP. (photo: courtesy Pavek Museum)

Anchors Pat Miles, Colleen Needles, Mark Rosen (sports) and Don Shelby. Miles has anchored on WCCO and KARE, Needles on WCCO and KSTP. Mark Rosen has been a fixture on WCCO sports for decades. Don Shelby moved from investigative reporting to anchor WCCO's TV news as the successful heir to Dave Moore. Miles and Shelby have also been heard on WCCO radio, while Needles heads up her own production company. (photos: courtesy Pavek Museum)

KARE News teams from the '80s included Tom Ryther, Diana Pierce, Paul Magers, Kirsten Lindquist, Paul Douglas, Randy Shaver, Barry ZeVan, John Bachmann and Joan Steffend. (photo: courtesy KARE 11)

KARE-11's news team in 2007 featured Randy Shaver, Julie Nelson, Mike Pomeranz, Diana Pierce and Belinda Jensen. (photo: courtesy KARE 11)

Chuck Knapp and Michael J. Douglas dominated morning drive time on KS95 in the '80s.
(photo: courtesy Pavek Museum)

Radio
Minnesota Tunes In

I t was Labor Day in Minnesota, Sept. 4, 1922. The new
Farmer-Labor Party was on the rise, spurred on by the
ongoing Shopmen's Strike of 1922, which included 8,000
railroad workers in the Twin Cities. From the pulpits, there was
talk of the effects of Prohibition—the advent of the speakeasy
and of "loose morals." Up in Cass Lake County, they founded
that day the tiny city of Boy River. Throughout the state, county
fair winners had traveled to St. Paul, where the Minnesota State
Fair had opened its doors for the season the day before, offering
free admission, as it would for 11 more years.

With all that going on this particular Labor Day,
probably few knew (or cared) that a tiny radio station called
WLAG, "The Call of the North," signed on with 500 watts in
studios on the sixth floor of a tiny hotel overlooking Loring
Park in Minneapolis. It just wasn't a big deal. But it would be.
By year's end, nine radio stations would be broadcasting in
Minnesota, including WBAD (owned by the *Minneapolis Journal*),
WAAL (owned by the *Minneapolis Morning Tribune*) and WBAH
(owned by the Dayton Co.). In 1923, that list would include the
forerunner to WDGY (a "jewelry and optical station" founded
by Dr. George Young, whose initials spelled D-G-Y) and the
forerunner to KSTP (founded by Stanley E. Hubbard).

It all began when two entrepreneurs enchanted with the
new ham crystal radio sets founded the Cutting and Washington
Radio Corp. of Minneapolis, hoping to start a station and create

a market for its sets. Nine Minnesota companies—including Northwestern National Bank and Donaldsons Department Store—helped pay the way the first year for WLAG, which broadcast classical music and live reports from U of M football games. In 1924, Washburn Crosby Co. of Minneapolis acquired the station as a marketing tool in its flour war with Pillsbury. In October, the station's call letters were changed to WCCO (for Washington Crosby Co.), "The Gold Medal Station."

On March 4, 1925, WCCO boasted a 5,000-watt transmitter on the site of an old chicken farm in Anoka, and that night broadcast President Coolidge's inaugural address. The station's broadcast that night made crystal radios obsolete. The new signal could be received only on the new tube radios, and consumers everywhere were buying them en masse as the radio revolution swept the country. In Minnesota, listeners were transfixed. In Duluth that year, WEBC upgraded its year-old 50-watt station to a whopping 100 watts. WHRM (the Rosedale Hospital station) launched that year and would eventually evolve into WTCN (Twin Cities Newspapers, a joint venture between the *St. Paul Pioneer Press* and *Minneapolis Tribune*). In 1926, KBRF signed on in Fergus Falls.

In 1928, KSTP was on the job, a merger between radio stations KFOY and WAMD ("Where All Minneapolis Dances," broadcasting live dance music from a local ballroom). According to *Radio Digest*: "It was Calvin Coolidge, sitting in Washington as the nation's chief executive in 1928, who pressed a gold key at his study in the White House to start the KSTP transmitter and sent this powerful station on the ether waves into its inaugural program on March 28 of that year."

It was the first radio station to be completely supported by income generated by running advertisements.

In 1929, WCCO cranked up power to 50,000 watts, and the Federal Radio Commission chose WCCO as a "clear channel" station, which gave it special status and freedom from signal interference in the nighttime skies. Now, WCCO could reach out into rural areas, and was often heard many states away. It became the most powerful station in the Northwest. In the 1930s, Cedric Adams was a familiar voice in Minnesota homes via WCCO, and on stormy winter mornings, families huddled around their radios, listening to him read the long list of school closings. (In later decades, Boone and Erickson would have this duty, and we all tuned in with fingers crossed to see if we'd be granted a snow day.) An airline pilot once remarked that, at night, he knew when Adams' 10 p.m. news was over because he would see lights in homes across the region go out at once.

By then, KSTP was occupying the entire 12th floor of the Saint Paul hotel. KSTP had 150 full-time staff, a full-time symphony orchestra and laid claim to the largest library west of New York. KSTP's old transmitter that Coolidge inaugurated had been replaced with a new 50,000-watt unit.

Among the many stations signing on in the 1930s were KROC in Rochester, WMFT in Hibbing and KCLD in St. Cloud. In 1939, Duluth's WEBC became the first station west of Chicago to venture into new FM radio technology, building the first FM transmitter in the area, long before FM's time.

In 1940, KWLM in Willmar and WLOL in the Twin Cities were on the air. In 1944, there were 18 radio stations in the state, six in the Twin Cities. (In 1948, WEBC Duluth was still trying to make that newfangled FM catch on, this time by "buscasting," installing FM receivers and speakers into 11 city buses and trolleys. After riders complained about being a captive audience, the Duluth Transit Authority killed the broadcasts. With the advent of television, WEBC would give up on the whole crazy idea of FM and abandon the FM dial in 1950. WEBC-AM remained. Today WEBC is on dial position 560 AM, broadcasting sports on The Fan Network.)

A new Minnesota radio station came on air every four months on average in the 1950s, according to Minnesota Broadcasters Assoc. In Detroit Lakes in 1951, Roger Awsumb started work as DJ and program director at KDLM before moving to the Twin Cities and into television. (On television, he would become famous with kids at lunchtime for 19 years as the lovable Casey Jones. In the mid-'80s, Awsumb would return north, and back to his radio roots, and join the staff of KLKS-FM as host, entertaining cabin-goers and residents in Breezy Point.)

Back in the Twin Cities in 1951, KDWB began life at 1590 on the AM dial as WCOW, playing "Western" and old-time music and signing on each day with a cowbell. The format failed, and in 1957 WCOW became WISK, a female-oriented station, on 630 kHz. Again, the format bombed. The station was sold to Crowell-Collier Broadcasting Co., which changed the format to top 40, and the call sign to KDWB. At last—by 1959, the bumbling WCOW was set up to succeed as KDWB.

The timing was right. Nationwide, teens were lured into the new top-40 concept by the arrival of the transistor radio. The idea of an affordable portable radio was a huge asset for radio stations wanting to attract youth.

Now KDWB was poised to go toe-to-toe with WDGY, the mighty "Weegee," which had been playing a pop music format for a few years. This was still on the AM dial, of course. (On his engaging website www.robsherwood.com, which is filled with area top-40 radio recollections, former Twin Cities radio DJ Rob Sherwood writes of the time: "The FM revolution had already started, but we were too stupid to recognize that AM top-40 radio was as good as dead. We didn't even know it was sick.")

WCCO-AM continued to dominate the market. But through the '60s and '70s, WDGY battled KDWB for young listeners, with the help of DJs such as True Don Bleu, Johnny Canton, Lance "Tac" Hammer, Jim Dandy, Jim Reed and Gene Leader (who would go on to become Mean Gene Okerlund of pro wrestling announcer fame). The competition resulted in some of the best promotions ever sponsored by local radio stations, according to many in the industry. Things heated up.

In the early-'60s, KDWB won the dubious distinction of being the first station in the country to be fined by the FCC for exceeding authorized nighttime power. The station paid $10,000 for the offense. In 1963, according to the St. Louis Park Historical Society website, "WDGY DJ Bill Diehl was the emcee at a Halloween dance at the St. Louis Park Roller Rink featuring The Trashmen, who had released their national smash hit, 'Surfin' Bird,' earlier that month. Expecting about 800 kids, an estimated 2,100 showed up. The enthusiastic crowd shattered the building's glass front wall, and reinforcements were sent for from the local constabulary."

When The Beatles came to town on Aug. 21, 1965, WDGY was granted preferential access and the opportunity to display WDGY call letters on Beatles microphones during the interview. KDWB fought for on-air presence by prefacing their live questions, with "KDWB wants to know."

By 1974, the AM dial in the Twin Cities was crowded with rock stations. KDWB, WDGY and KSTP all battled for the local top-40 radio crown. But it was one station, WYOO ("Super U100"), that would imbed itself into the collective memories of a generation.

U100 was on the air for only two years in the '70s, simulcast on 980 and 101.3, but it remains one of the best-remembered and infamous chapters in Minnesota radio history. Rock music and memorable DJs (including Masa Kincaid—the "fox that rocks"—and "the breakfast buddy club" of Jerry St. James and Michael J. Donuts) shook up the Northland, and kids latched onto the new station with a passion. The existing station had been playing oldies and soft-pop to an audience of middle-aged women. But ratings were low and owners threatened to sell until General Manager Mike Sigelman and Program Director/DJ Rob Sherwood made a radical change at the Minnesota State Fair. According to an article by J.R. Lonto on www.studioz7.com:

On the afternoon of August 26, 1974 milling crowds strolled past the WYOO booth at the State Fair, paying little attention as Rob Sherwood played moldy oldies from Lesley Gore, the Shirelles and the Critters when he abruptly stopped the music, declaring "I can't take any more of this ... from now on it's boogie!" As he played Joe Cocker's Woodstock performance of "With A Little Help From My Friends" he promised there'd be "no more turkey records."... The radio booth that had been playing quaint oldies was suddenly blasting hard rock. People were taking notice, especially teens bored with the local top-40 offerings. ... And the audience mushroomed like a nuclear explosion.

A recording of the U100 format switch can be heard at www.radiotapes.com, along with comments by listeners and radio personnel who recall the days of U100 with authority, including this anonymous post:

The final hour of U100 is, in my opinion, one of the most overlooked and under appreciated pieces of Twin Cities radio history. We all remember WDGY's switch to County in 1978 and WLOL's signoff in 1990. But few have instant recollection of U100's 'swan song.' ... Unfortunately, there just wasn't enough audience to support four Top 40 stations.

Meanwhile, over at KSTP-AM, Chuck Knapp and Charlie Bush, along with a new rock format, brought the station from 13th place to second place in the Twin Cities radio ratings, according to J.R. Lonto. When Knapp left in 1976 (returning to KSTP-FM three years later), Bush was teamed with 22-year-old John Hines (who would go on to be paired with Bob Berglund on WLOL, and later, reign for more than a decade on K102-FM's morning show).

FM took over. A top 40 station, WLOL-FM, signed on in 1981 and gave KDWB-AM a run for its money. In 1981, WLTE evolved from the former WCCO-FM. Michael J. Douglas and Chuck Knapp—aka "Knapp and Donuts"—were the stars of KS95 as the morning team.

KSTP-AM evolved into its current news/talk format by 1979, and through the years featured hosts including Jesse Ventura, Tom Barnard, Don Vogel, Joe Soucheray, James Lileks, Pat Reusse, Barbara Carlson, Tom Mischke and Jason Lewis.

As the '80s wound down, WCCO was the last musical AM station in the market, and practically in the nation, that could claim to be the market leader, ahead of WLTE (102.9) and Hubbard's KS95. Rock continued to do well in the Twin Cities in the '80s. KQRS was in the top three by the end of the decade, far ahead of rivals Cities 97 and KJJO. (But Cities 97 had won the hearts of Minnesotans for its annual compilation CD, *The Cities Sampler*, so popular that customers camp out at local Target stores on the night of release. The last few volumes have sold out within a few hours.)

In the '90s, WCCO turned to a music and talk format, and stayed No. 1 most of the decade, eventually pushed off the hill by KQRS (whose morning host Tom Barnard lived earlier radio lives at WDGY as "Cat Man" and at KSTP-AM).

Over at 1130 AM, in 1991, the historic call letters WDGY were put to rest, and in their place came the letters "KFAN" to herald a new sports-talk format. "The Fan" would now lay claim to the title of oldest radio station in the state.

Country K102-FM did well through the '90s, and in mid-decade, along with WBOB and K00L-108, was acquired by Chancellor Media. Following loosened ownership limits in 1996, Chancellor owned six stations in the market—K102, KOOL-108, Cities 97, KDWB, WRQC and KFAN. Other owners in the market were ABC and CBS Radio, along with the smaller

Hubbard and Cargill. Chancellor eventually became part of Clear Channel and CBS Radio merged into Infinity.

Minnesota radio continued to evolve. Alternative radio, specialty formats, even pirate radio stations have been found on the dial in the '90s and beyond. Beat Radio, co-created by Minnesota programmer and DJ Alan Freed, was perhaps the most famous of the pirates. Freed went on to broadcast the Beat Radio dance music format from a number of different stations, a webcast and satellite radio.

Now, in the face of new media, Minnesota radio stations are reaching out to listeners via new methods, including webcasts. (Go to www.northpine.com for a list of links of radio webcasts for stations in the Twin Cities, Ely, Duluth, Glenwood, Grand Rapids, St. Cloud, Mankato and Morris.) New technology also keeps the past alive. Cedric Adams is long gone, but his voice and others live on through websites like www.radiotapes.com (which includes a link to a very funny blooper reel from the '50s of Adams cracking up on air) and www.twincitiesradioairchecks.com. Radio personalities continue to re-invent themselves: In his third decade in Minnesota radio, John Hines in early 2007 moved from country K102 to talker KTLK (100.3 FM) as morning host.

Nearly 90 years after the forerunner to WCCO made its first radio broadcast on Labor Day, area radio stations will continue to mark their modern Labor Days from their broadcast booths at the Minnesota State Fair, still seeking, after all these years, new ways to capture new listeners. Let's keep listening. Just in case. Somewhere along the way, maybe there will be a new U100 or Cedric Adams to turn our heads. 📡

Johnny Canton and a host of others led the AM rock 'n' roll radio wars of the '60s between KDWB and WDGY in the Twin Cities. Canton later was heard on WLTE and seen on *Bowling For Dollars*. (photo: courtesy Pavek Museum)

Howard Viken   Rog Erickson   Joyce Lamont   Maynard Speece   Bob DeHaven   Jim Hill

"The Morning Crew"
Of The People You Know At
WCCO RADIO
Dial 8-3-0

WCCO dominated the airwaves with news, humor, farm and weather reports featuring Cedric Adams and The Morning Crew. (photo: courtesy Pavek Museum)

Charlie Boone and Roger Erickson got big ratings hosting mornings on WCCO-AM. Erickson was also the voice of Minnesota Gopher games. (photo: courtesy Pavek Museum)

Steve Cannon worked in both radio and TV across the dial and dominated evening drive on WCCO Radio until he retired. Cannon was famous for his cast of characters Ma Linger, Backlash LaRue and Morgan Mundane. (photo: courtesy Pavek Museum)

Herb Carneal, Halsey Hall and Ray Scott teamed on radio and TV for the early Minnesota Twins broadcasts. (photo: courtesy Pavek Museum)

Jimmy Reed and Tac Hammer, left, in a promotional photo with disc jockeys from KDWB. Right, icons Rob Sherwood and True Don Bleu on KDWB in the '70s. Sherwood later defected to "Super" U100. (photos: courtesy Timothy D. Kehr and Rob Sherwood)

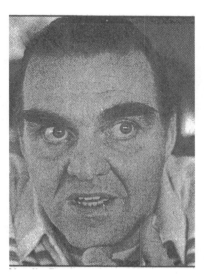

Bill Diehl and Charlie Bush were heard across the dial. Diehl hosted The Beatles at Met Stadium for WDGY, sold cars on WCCO for Wally McCarthy and wrote for the *St. Paul Pioneer Press*. Charlie Bush formed a highly rated team with John Hines. (photos: courtesy Pavek Museum)

Don Vogel yucked it up on KSTP with imitations, "phantom caller" Tom Mischke, Pat Reusse, Joe Soucheray and John MacDougall. (photo: courtesy Pavek Museum)

Bob Yates was a ratings leader for KSTP then KFAN. Ruth Koscielak was a daytime fixture on WCCO-AM for many years. (photos: courtesy Pavek Museum and *Mpls/St.Paul* Magazine)

Steve Cochran, here with members of Journey, was a fabled jock on KDWB-FM and currently resides on WGN Chicago. (photo courtesy WGN)

Chad Hartman and Dan Bareirro first together and then on separate shows, helped KFAN sports radio gain listeners in the Twin Cities and statewide through syndication. (photo: courtesy Clear Channel Radio)

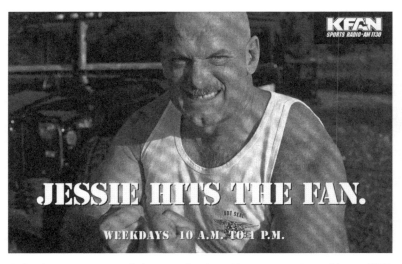

Before he was governor and after wrestling, Jesse Ventura spent time talking on KSTP and KFAN in the Twin Cities. (photo: courtesy Clear Channel Radio)

Dan Donovan, here with John Lennon, has been popular across the Twin Cities dial. His distinct voice and comic wit have endured for decades.
(photo: courtesy Pavek Museum)

John Hines and Bob Bergland combined to make WLOL a powerhouse in the Twin Cities.

Tom Barnard, center, with friends at a Metrodome tribute, has led the KQRS morning show in the Twin Cities with various sidekicks including Terri Traen since the 1980s. Barnard's quick wit and sense of humor has led him to the top of Minnesota radio. In previous lives across the dial, Barnard was a DJ known at "The Cat." (photo: courtesy KQRS)

The WAYL car appeared at many events. (photo: courtesy Pavek Museum)

Greater Minnesota Dials In

KRJB Ada KKIN Aitken **KASM Albany** KATE Albert Lea
KXRA Alexandria KAUS Austin **KBHP Bemidji** KBLB
Baxter **KSCR Benson** KBEW Blue Earth **KLIZ Brainerd**
KLKS Breezy Point **WKLK Cloquet** KDAL KQDS KBBR
KTCO KUMD WAKX WEBC Duluth **KBOT Detroit Lakes**
WELY Ely **WEVE Eveleth** KJJK Fergus Falls **KKCQ Fosston**
KAXE KOZY Grand Rapids **WNMT Hibbing** KARP Hutchin-
son **KBHW International Falls** TLF Little Falls **KLQL**
Luverne KLQP Madison **KRJM Mahnomen** KEEZ KTOE
Mankato **KKCK Marshall** KDMA Montevideo **KVOX KTLA**
Moorhead KBEK Mora **KNUJ New Ulm** KDIO Ortonville
KOWO Owatonna KTIG Pequot Lakes **WCMP Pine City**
KFIL Preston **KPRM Park Rapids** WQPM Princeton **KWNG**
Red Wing KLGR Redwood Falls **KOLM KRCH KROC**
KWWK KNXR Rochester KCAJ Roseau **KKJM Sauk Rapids**
KJOE Slayton **KNSG Springfield** WWJO KKSR KMXK KNSI
St. Cloud **KRBI St. Peter** WMGT Stillwater **KKAQ Thief**
River Falls KKWS Wadena **KKWQ Warroad** KWOM Water-
town **KDJS KQIC Willmar KDOM Windom** KWNO Winona
KITN Worthington

Elmo, *Sesame Street* and children's programming have entertained and educated thousands on Minnesota's public television stations. (photo: courtesy tpt)

Public TV and Radio
Educating, Entertaining, Coming of Age

M ention the words "public broadcasting" and many might
think of the ubiquitous pledge drive banter ("If you
call in now...")—and requisite premiums (do I really *need* the
grizzled faces of Gerry and The Pacemakers and others of the
bygone pop world, singing their old hits, if I call in now?). But
in Minnesota, the sight and sound of the public airwaves readily
transcend the public TV and radio stereotypes, simply because
both are consistently so good—and diverse and necessary.

Today, almost everyone knows that "it's been a quiet
week in Lake Wobegon" for more than 30 years, courtesy of
Minnesota Public Radio (MPR, now in its fourth decade).
And in 2007 many were reminded that the cameras have been
rolling over at Twin Cities Public Television (TPT/KTCA) for
half a century. Similar landmark anniversaries have occurred
at other public radio and television stations, even down to the
college level: KUMD at the University of Minnesota Duluth in
2007 celebrated its 50th year on the air, and KVSC-FM at St.
Cloud State University noted its 40th anniversary.

The recently organized Independent Public Radio
(IPR) group of Minnesota stations—often overshadowed by
the bigger public outlets—remains the second-largest public
radio network in the state "and one of the largest public
radio networks of its kind in the United States," including 12
independently licensed and managed local stations across the
state. According to IPR's website, its collective signal covers

nine-tenths of the state and 92 percent of the population. It claims almost 300,000 listeners, from the mighty KAXE-FM in Grand Rapids to the heart and soul of the Twin Cities, KMOJ-FM (serving the African-American community) to KBEM-FM (known for its live traffic reports for the Twin Cities, its jazz programming by north side Minneapolis high school students, a long-running *Bluegrass Saturday Morning* show hosted by Phil Nussbaum and other terrific acoustic shows).

The state's larger leading media organizations, however, like "Channel 2," as it has been more fondly known since it came into its own, have added substantially to the proverbial "quality of life" equation. And their impact readily extends beyond Minnesota's borders. TPT has over its 50 seasons been creating top-line features like the Academy Awards-nominated *Hoop Dreams* (1995), the Emmy Award-winning kids' science show *Newton's Apple* (which ran for 15 seasons nationally) and other high-impact television, including Suze Orman's *The Laws of Money, The Lessons of Life.*

Such hard-earned longevity for programs like these on public TV and others on radio are not hard to understand: Minnesota is home to some of the most powerful and innovative public broadcast programming, personalities, producers and empire builders anywhere in the country.

Public TV productions have simply become must-see TV for thousands of Minnesotans, from the "up north" profiles of the places and peoples featured regularly on the *Venture North* program in Duluth at WDSE-TV to Lakeland Public Television (Channel 9) in Brainerd, which offers the only nightly newscast in that area, making it a community asset in the truest sense. The 23-year-old *Almanac* show in the Twin Cities is the area's most-watched public TV program, regularly tackling politics, punditry and policymaking every Friday night. Hosts Cathy Wurzer (also the morning host at MPR's *Morning Edition*) and the guy with all the scarves, WCCO's capitol reporter, Eric Eskola, have been on *Almanac* since '96 and '86 respectively, and also are married in real life.

For all of its color and personality through the years, the 50-year-old station has somewhat practical, black-and-white roots. Its first show on Sept. 16, 1957—in black and white—was an educational Spanish class with Don Miguel, broadcast from the University of Minnesota. In its early years, virtually all programming emanated from upper academia and the public school system—theatrical dramas, dance events, ag extension courses, choirs (including the traditional broadcast of the St. Olaf Christmas Concert, which has been playing on and off since 1961). For a long time, beginning in 1957, public TV here and around the country often meant only "educational TV." In fact, Channel 2 was incorporated as a nonprofit entity as Twin City Area Educational Television (ETV) in 1955 until it finally became part of PBS (Public Broadcasting Service) in 1974.

According to Brendan Henahan, the station's in-house historian and *Almanac*'s executive producer since 1984, Channel 2's reluctance (or stubbornness) to join PBS hinged on General Manager John Schwarzwalder. Henahan says in a fun and insightful Top 10 list he prepared for the 50th, *Ten Things You Probably Don't Know About TPT*: "For many years KTCA was known for its antagonism towards PBS and the CPB [the Corporation for Public Broadcasting].... In 1974 there

was exactly one public station that was not a member of PBS...
and that was KTCA." Henahan notes that the GM blasted the
mother ship every chance he got and earned the nickname
"PBS Vice President of Dissent."

Schwarzwalder was also a serious fan of theater and
pushed for a station-run theater in the mid-'60s. He got his
wish in 1969 when KTCA negotiated a year's lease on what
is now the History Theatre in downtown St. Paul and put on
a season of plays. Hugh Beaumont (the dad in *Leave It To
Beaver*) was hired to direct. The reality of this grand notion
probably wasn't the legacy anyone affiliated with the idea had
in mind—or any other early believers in public TV, for that
matter: The plays got mediocre reviews, the theater lost money
and, Henahan writes, when the station put on a production
of *Macbeth*, "the star died on stage opening night. The losses
caused by the theater failure caused the station to lay off 25
percent of its work force in 1970 and forced KTCI off the air
for the entire summer."

Things changed dramatically, this time for the better,
in 1976 when Bill Kobin took over the reins. Kobin developed
an aggressive brand of programming that packaged local arts,
entertainment, news and eventually, under Executive Producer
of Programming Gerry Richmond and Executive Producer
Catherine Allen, powerful nationally recognized specials such
as in-depth profiles of *Benjamin Franklin*, painter Grant Wood,
Liberty! The American Revolution (with MiddleMarch Films) and
other award-winning pieces like *Hoop Dreams* (the basketball
documentary about inner-city Chicago kids hoping for a lane out
of the ghetto, done in collaboration with Kartemquin Films).

Kobin instituted the NightTimes Variety series in 1980, five nights of engaging and often surprisingly brilliant locally produced television, among the shows *Night Times Magazine*, *Variety* (which featured a wealth of local, national and international bands and musicians) and *Weekend* (the forerunner to *Almanac*, which debuted in 1984 with hosts Jan Smaby and the late Joe Summers, a Ramsey County judge). Henahan says KTCA is just one of a couple dozen public television stations around the country that produces a "healthy dose" of national and local programming but gets the highest Nielson ratings of all PBS stations.

Among its other noteworthy headlines, the station was the first PBS station nationally to broadcast in color in 1967. As for its *program-interruptus* pledge drives: Well, if viewers were tuned in around the early-'70s, they might have been able to lunch with one of Hollywood's film legends—for the right kind of pledge, Henahan observes. "In 1972, one of the items for bid on the station's Action Auction was a lunch date with actor Cary Grant. Apparently Grant came to St. Paul often as a board member of Faberge and was a big supporter of public broadcasting."

You probably won't find a bigger, more influential— and occasionally more controversial—Minnesota supporter of its public airwaves than MPR's William "Bill" Kling, an empire builder in every sense. Alongside National Public Radio— which MPR helped found in 1970—MPR is the most important public radio station in the country. And one of the most creative, producing national hits under its banner, American Public Media Group (APMG, which includes MPR), like *The Splendid Table*, with host Lynne Rossetto Kasper, *Speaking of*

Faith, Marketplace, St. Paul Sunday and many others, totaling
20 shows, including *Prairie Home* and *The Jazz Image*, hosted by
the legendary Leigh Kamman, who celebrated 60 years in the
industry in 2003 and is still going strong in his 80s!

Kling, who has been honored with many of broadcast's
highest awards, including an Edward R. Murrow Award, serves
as president and CEO of APMG. Ask him to list MPR's key
benchmarks and he says, "There is one nearly every month." His
scorecard includes: the Corporation for Public Broadcasting grant
to subsidize local news programming for five years in 1973 and
the opening of its first major production center in 1979, followed
by an expansion in 2006; the nation's first radio reading service
for the blind in 1968; hiring Keillor in 1969 and purchasing and
refurbishing the World Theater (now the Fitzgerald) in 1985,
where *Prairie Home* played for many years; founding the Rivertown
Trading Co. and Greenspring Co. in 1983; and establishing The
Current in 2005, which significantly boosted the local music scene
with its appealing array of music-wise DJs.

Not bad for a station started in 1967 by Benedictine
monks at St. John's University. But among the many
achievements of what was once just a college radio station lie
some well-publicized controversies, including the operation of
the Rivertown Trading Co., a direct mail catalog which was a
for-profit entity used to fund MPR's nonprofit operations, and
the acquisition of Southern California Public Radio (SCPR),
which reaches 14 million people in the Los Angeles area.

Other media and the state legislature took a hard look
at Kling's Rivertown deal, a hard enough analysis, anyway, to
force a sale of the enterprise to Dayton Hudson in 1998. The

radio giant, whose role models or personal heroes include
Frank Stanton of CBS, Gary Comer of Lands' End and Jon
Lovelace of Capital Group (Kling is a director of seven fund
boards around the country, including Capital Group), brushes
aside criticism of the Rivertown events: "It provided tens of
millions of dollars of profits to support MPR, and it provided a
$100 plus million permanent endowment for Minnesota Public
Radio/American Public Media." It also reportedly poured a
little money into Kling's growing portfolio.

If Kling is one of the nation's crowned kings of public
radio, Keillor is its erudite court jester, in-house Will Rogers,
Minnesota storyteller-in-residence and the unlicensed poetic
purveyor of Scandinavian stereotypes. He's been sweetly and
subversively coming into homes every Saturday afternoon with
his famous *Prairie Home* broadcast. Like old, usually reliable
clockwork, he unloads highbrow goods and more familiar
fare: opera singers from the Met and symphony orchestras,
mixed with unwashed bluegrass groups, Celtic pipers, funky
singer-songwriters, yodelers, gospel singers, joke tellers, known
and unknown musical talent, *faux* sponsors like The Ketchup
Advisory Board and Powdermilk Biscuits, and his inspired
weekly monologue, The News from Lake Wobegon.

His cast over the years has featured Dudley Riggs
alumnus Sue Scott, WCCO radio's on-again-off-again Tim
Russell, sound effects aces Tom Keith and Fred Newman, MVP
pianist Rich Dworksy and the house band, Guy's All Star Shoe
Band, which has backed a Who's Who lineup of popular music
artists from all genres – and from all over the world. Keillor
modeled *PHC* on the old Grand Old Opry broadcasts, but

there's a bit of the eclectic Ed Sullivan showman in the Anoka-raised homeboy (born Gary Edward Keillor).

The self-described "Old Scout" humbly sprang up first over KSJR-FM at St. John's back in the day with a morning program called simply, *The Morning Show*. It usually defied description but was not without defining moments like The Beach Boys' "Help Me Rhonda" followed by Vivaldi. Keillor eventually handed off that show to Dale Connelly and Jim Ed Poole (nee Tom Keith, with whom he shared the morning mic). Since Keillor's departure and Connelly's arrival in 1983, the two have done a remarkable job creating their own *Morning Show* (now on The Current every weekday).

In 2006, the legendary filmmaker Robert Altman made a movie (ultimately a meditation on death) about *A Prairie Home Companion,* Altman's last in a string of great films that included *Nashville, 3 Women, The Player* and many more. A new movie from Keillor's world is rumored to be in the works. But so far, the locals at the Chatterbox Café aren't talking.

While the giants of MPR and KTCA loom large in the history of Minnesota's—and the nation's—public airwaves, there's no denying the impact of other longstanding community resources of the air. KFAI-FM in the Twin Cities, Fresh Air Radio, which boasts "A new radio station every hour," lives up to the claim by serving the south Minneapolis area (with some reach into St. Paul and the suburbs) with more diversified programming than anywhere in the state. Shows by and for the growing Somali and Hispanic communities, music from ancient Persia, Afro-Caribbean, folk, funk, hip hop, swing, R&B, all variations of rock, country, public affairs shows, shows about writers, the gay community, art—you name it, Fresh Air has it.

But for sheer underground music tenacity and rock 'n' roll moxie, you won't find a cooler radio vibe than the one put out during daylight hours only, at the University of Minnesota's Radio K on the AM dial, a successor to the student-run stations WMMR and later KUOM, whose respective histories date back to 1912 and 1948. Among WMMR's and KUOM's noteworthy broadcasters were Keillor and one Billy Golfus. Golfus' KUOM work, where he was a media producer, received numerous national awards for compelling radio documentaries and investigative pieces. He also created "Real Rock and Roll Radio" in the '80s, what may well be the forerunner of Radio K.

But Golfus became even better known when he nearly died in a Vespa crash, and after a month-long coma, slowly recovered from his brain injury and eventually made a television documentary about his accident—and "disability"—with ITVS called *When Billy Broke His Head*. It won prizes at 27 film festivals and played on TV in 17 countries. It also earned him an Emmy nomination for his script, a Guggenheim fellowship for filmmaking, and a consulting stint at Dreamworks SKG for the film, *Lookout*.

In the land of 10,000 broadcast towers, that kind of blunt force resourcefulness, personal ingenuity and determined creativity that Golfus demonstrated underscores much of the public programming emanating from the Loon state, thanks to the long march of those who do all the work. Most of them remain as invisible as the frequencies they broadcast on. But ultimately they leave an indelible mark on Minnesota, its people, history and culture, and often the rest of the nation, too. (•))

In the '60s KTCA hosted *Inquiry*, a local news forum, and *Live From (The New) Guthrie Theater*. (photos: courtesy tpt)

Action Auction from KTCA's studios near the Minnesota State Fair in St. Paul filled the airwaves from the '60s to '80s. (photos: courtesy tpt)

KTCA logos through the years. (photo: courtesy tpt)

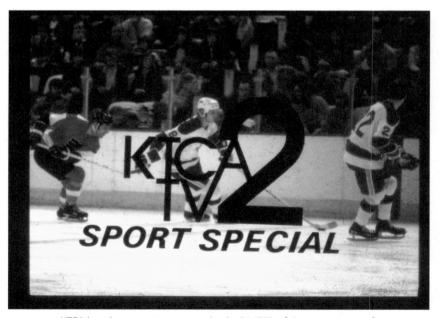

KTCA broadcast sports programming in the 1970s. (photo: courtesy tpt)

Almanac, here with Jan Smaby, has been an longtime statewide forum for history, politics, sports and pop culture. (photo: courtesy tpt)

A Prairie Home Companion, with Garrison Keillor, live from The Fitzgerald Theatre in St. Paul, has grown from Minnesota Public Radio to movies and national fame. (photo: courtesy PHC, Dana Nye photographer)

Mpls. Magazine evolved into *Mpls.St. Paul* in the '70s.

Magazines
Land of 10,000 Stories

In the early days of Minnesota history, newspapers were the
primary news source, but magazines were the dominant
means of mass communication nationally. No doubt a few
Minnesotans waited eagerly for the postman to deliver their
first periodicals—the whole family taking turns reading *Saturday Evening Post* (first published in 1821); the more well-heeled
subscribing to *Harper's* or *Scribner's*; and the kids lapping up
Youth's Companion (1827-1929). Successful women's magazines such as *Godey's Lady's Book* (1830–1898) and *Ladies' Home
Journal* (1883) had large readerships and set the stage for
future magazines.

In the 1870s, Minnesota was growing quickly. The
spread of railroads helped make Minneapolis the gateway
to the northern plains, and flour milling put the city on the
map, with Minneapolis on its way to becoming the world
center of flour milling late in the century. So it's no surprise
that one of Minnesota's first periodicals was a national trade
publication for flour millers. When the first edition of the
Northwestern Miller rolled off the press in 1873, Minneapolis-
based Miller Publishing Co. became one of the first specia-
lized business publishing companies in America. According
to *A History of Minneapolis: Printing and Publishing*, an over-
view by Minneapolis Public Library staff: "*The Miller* served
as an important news medium for the cereal processing
industry and was long considered the international aris-

tocrat of trade and business publications." Miller Publishing
is still in operation, now in Minnetonka, publishing
business-to-business magazines. Other early Minneapolis
publications were also business periodicals—*The Bellman,*
American Bar and *American Worker.*

Just two years after *National Geographic* made its debut,
the University of Minnesota's alumni magazine (now titled
Minnesota) began publishing in 1901. The past issues of the
magazine are housed in the alumni association's library, the
volumes from the early 1900s well-thumbed and brittle, but
yielding a rich record of the time.

By the first decade of the 20th century, while national
popular magazines began to become not only a pleasurable
pursuit but also a powerful medium with the ability to effect
change and social reform, here at home, the lumber industry was evolving—moving from Stillwater to Minneapolis
to northern Minnesota, feeding Minnesota's printing and
publishing industry, which would remain one of the state's
key industries.

In 1915, the Minnesota Historical Society began
publishing *Minnesota History,* a quarterly magazine still in
publication. In 1940, four years after *Life* magazine launched
nationally, the Hennepin County Historical Society started
Hennepin County History (now *Hennepin History*), which began
life as a publication of the Work Projects Administration.

A U of M humor magazine, *Ski-U-Mah,* was published
from about 1930 to 1950. It launched the career of novelist
and scriptwriter Max Shulman, who later wrote the stories that
became the television program *The Many Loves of Dobie Gillis.*

By the '60s, magazines mirrored the times, and mass-market general-interest publications were giving way to a variety of special-interest magazines. Meanwhile, surveys found that about 60 percent of Americans regularly read a magazine, and magazine circulations reached millions. It was prime time for Minnesota's premier magazines to launch.

Mention "Minnesota magazines" and most will think of two titles—*Minnesota Monthly*, which began publishing in 1967, and *Mpls.St. Paul Magazine*, which launched in 1971 as *MPLS Magazine*. Since their inception, these magazines have survived competitors (from the long-defunct *Twin Cities Magazine* to the current *Rake* and *Metro* magazines) to reign as the glossy magazine market leaders.

Minnesota Monthly, published by Greenspring Media Group (formerly Minnesota Monthly Publications, a for-profit subsidiary of Greenspring Co., which falls under the American Public Media Group umbrella) is published for upscale readers including Minnesota Public Radio members, who make up more than half the magazine's subscription base. The company also publishes *Midwest Home*, various contract visitor and convention magazines, *Where Twin Cities* and national titles such as *Drinks, Carat* and *Real Food*.

Mpls.St. Paul magazine, published by MSP Communications, has become one of the top city magazines in the country. Founded by Burt Cohen (who would sell his company twice in coming years), the company also publishes *Twin Cities Business, Minnesota Law & Politics, Mpls.St.Paul Wedding Guide* and numerous custom publications for clients including Northwest Airlines, IBM, the Minnesota Twins,

Carlson-Wagonlit Travel, Thrivent Financial for Lutherans
and Minnesota Golf Assoc.

In 1973, local publisher Bill Dorn bought *Corporate
Report Minnesota*, a 5-year-old tabloid, and converted it to a
monthly magazine. He would later sell the magazine to *Twin
Cities Reader* publisher Mark Hopp, and the magazine would
be closed in the '90s when Hopp's company was acquired by
American City Business Journals.

In the early-'80s, *Lake Superior Magazine* launched.
The national *Utne Reader* (now simply *Utne*) was founded in
1984 by Eric Utne, reprinting articles from more than 2,000
alternative media sources. The publication was sold in 2006
to Ogden Publications.

In 1987, Steve Adams (son of broadcaster and newspa-
perman Cedric Adams) bought MSP Communications from
Burt Cohen, published for a few years, then sold it back to
Cohen. Also in the late-'80s, Mark Hopp started *Request*, a national music magazine for Musicland, which boasted the first
female editor of a national music pub, Susan Hamre.

Minnesota Journal of Law and Politics (now *Minnesota
Law and Politics*) launched in 1990. The magazine's website
sums it all up: "In its ... history, (*Law and Politics*) has been
accused of being too liberal, too conservative, too smart and
too sophomoric. But it's never been accused of being a bore.
Thus its slogan, 'Only our name is boring.' "

MSP Communications' *Twin Cities Business Monthly*
launched in the early-'90s, as did Metropolitan Media Group's
(MMG) *Minnesota Business Magazine*. MMG now also publishes
about 15 city lifestyle magazines for various metro communities.

In 1993, Duluth-based national *New Moon* magazine was launched by publisher Nancy Gruver, as a way of helping her then 11-year-old twin daughters "make the transition from girls to women."

In the mid-'90s, Cohen again sold his MSP Communications, this time to West Publishing's Vance Opperman, with MSP now under the Key Professional Media banner.

Brainerd-based *Lake Country Journal Magazine* began in 1996, the brainchild of publishers Chip and Jean Borkenhagen.

Upsize Minnesota, targeting small business with a how-to approach, launched in 2002, and continues on. *Women's Business Minnesota* launched in 2003, and competed in the business publication market until folding in January 2006.

In 2002, *City Pages* founders Tom Bartel and Kristin Henning reached for yet another piece of the Twin Cities magazine pie when they launched *Rake*, with a niche somewhere between the alternative weeklies and the glossy mega-monthlies. Four years later, Tiger Oak Publishing attempted to share that niche and launched *Metro*, a city magazine targeted at a younger audience not served by the old-guard glossies. A year later, in 2007, further south in Minnesota, *Rochester Magazine* got a new look and new website.

While the magazine industry struggles with competition from the internet and traditional media, periodical publishers continue to diversify, and specialty publications abound in Minnesota. One of the newest entries in the state's magazine market, Duluth-based Fladmark Publishing launched its national *Cabin Life* magazine, inviting readers: "Pull up a chair. Put your feet up. Don't answer the phone.

Imagine the sounds of traffic slowly yielding to the sounds surrounding the cabin."

Maple Grove-based Ehlert Publishing Group (since 1996 owned by California-based Affinity Group) publishes 15 national powersports-enthusiast magazines, targeted at readers who own motorcycles, personal watercraft, snowmobiles and all-terrain vehicles. General Mills continues publishing national recipe magazines. And as they did in the beginning of Minnesota publishing history when *Northwestern Miller* launched, national trade magazines published here are plentiful—from multiple titles published by the Industrial Fabrics Assoc. to *Food Service News* and *Franchise Times.*

The Minnesota Magazine and Publications Assoc. boasts 95 magazine publishing companies among its members, and its 2006 awards show demonstrated the scope of magazine pubishing in the state. *Experience Life,* published by Life Time Fitness, beat out the big city magazines to win top honors for overall excellence in the General Interest category for large-circulation magazines. Brainerd's *Lake Country Journal Magazine* took top honors for overall excellence in its class. Other Overall Excellence Gold Award winners included: Greenspring's *Drinks*; MSP Communications' *Twin Cities Business*; Rochester-based *Exhibitor Magazine*; U of M's *Minnesota*; and the *Carleton College Voice.*

To the relief of printers and publishers, the internet has not made magazines obsolete. But their role is certainly changing, and publishers are adapting to new challenges. Modern readers are more likely to read a chatty blog online by their favorite magazine writer than they are to wait by the mailbox to find out what's in the current issue. But that's OK. Even those readers likely find it more satisfying snuggling up with a good magazine than with a laptop, and if the stacks of glossies on the bookshelves and coffee tables of Minnesota homes and cabins are any indication, magazines are not going away anytime soon. (( ))

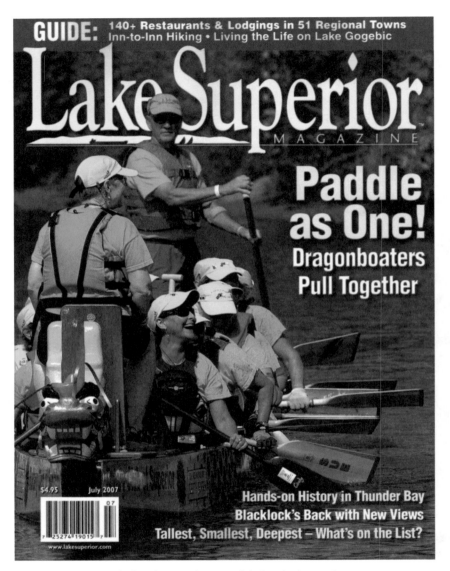

Lake Superior magazine covers Duluth and points north.

JANUARY 1985 $2.50

.Ordway Music Theatre

Centerpiece of a City Reborn

Twin Cities, part of Dorn Communications, was a 1980s city magazine success.

Minnesota Monthly past and present.

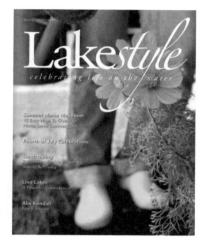

Minnesota lifestyle magazines from lakes to rivers, local to national.

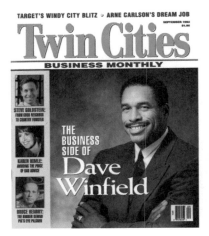
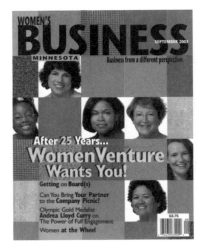

Minnesota business magazines through the years.

Clockwise from top left: Brian Anderson, Burt Cohen, Vance Opperman and Bill Dorn played critical roles in Minnesota magazines. Anderson, as the longtime editor of *Mpls.St. Paul* magazine, Cohen as publisher. Opperman moved from West Publishing to own *Mpls.St. Paul* and *Twin Cities Business Monthly*. He also provides commentary on KTCA. Bill Dorn owned *Corporate Report* and founded *Twin Cities* magazine.
(photos: courtesy MSP and 2 Bills Publishing)

Cheryl Johnson, aka "CJ," dishes Minnesota gossip about Prince, local TV personalities, national celebs and more in the *Star Tribune*. (photo: courtesy CJ)

Newspapers
The Scoop on Papers Past and Present

*"There is nothing more certain than that the interests of Minnesota
require an able and efficient press, to represent abroad our wants and
to set forth our situation, our resources and our advantages."*

–James A. Goodhue, publisher, *Minnesota Pioneer,* (the first newspaper
established in Minnesota), April 28, 1849

A publisher at a North Carolina city daily stood in front
of the newsroom and talked briefly about what impact a
new computer-based network called the internet might have
on the industry. It was the early-'90s. In the room was a young
reporter who would eventually move to Minneapolis and work
for the *Star Tribune.* The scribe shrugged. He wanted to get
back to work and make his deadline.

For more than 158 years, hundreds of Minnesota
newspapers have diligently met deadlines to deliver world
and local headlines and other features. Intensely competitive
for leading editorial content and sustaining advertising
dollars, generally newspapers lean one way or the other
politically. Although undercut by the rise of broadcasting
in the last century and currently in a deepening quandary
in this century because of the internet, it's hard to imagine
any community without the many voices stemming from
its daily, neighborhood and alternative newspapers, or the
many specialty papers catering to everything from feminism
and family to new age and the state's growing minority

communities, among them the Twin Cities' longstanding papers in the African-American community, *Insight* and *The Minnesota Spokesman Recorder*.

According to George S. Hage's *Newspapers on the Minnesota Frontier 1849-1860*, there were already three weekly papers touting the merits of the territory to settlers in the days of '49 and beating the drum of the political parties of the day. It would be roughly 10–20 years more before outstate papers like the *The Duluth News-Tribune* (established in 1869) or the *The St. Cloud Times* (1861) would be begin reporting. *Rochester Post Bulletin*, the third largest in the state, began in 1854 (although the paper was not named that until a merger of two presses in 1925).

News from these cities invariably reflected the good, bad and prosaic doings of the day. The June 16, 1920, front page of *The Duluth News Tribune* featured a wretched story and photograph about how three young African-American circus workers were hanged from a street pole by a seething mob for an alleged rape that was never proven, then thrown in unmarked graves until 1991.

The state's earliest newspapers, however, were filled with news that was much less dramatic, notes Hage, a former University of Minnesota professor of journalism. "Other functions—informing the community about itself and the outside world, mounting a watch on government, advertising goods and services, instructing and entertaining readers—got less attention from editors in the early years." By the 1940s in Minneapolis and as early as the '20s in St. Paul there were morning and afternoon editions of both dailies. Twin Citians had that luxury until the early-to-mid-'80s when the morning and afternoon editions at both papers merged into single morning papers.

The longtime owners of each enterprise during the 20th century were from out of town: The Cowles family in Minneapolis came originally from Des Moines, and the Ridder family in St. Paul heralded from New York. Before 2000, the biggest newspapers in the state also sowed great—if not occasionally controversial—benefits to the community.

According to a recent account of the *Star Tribune*'s history in the paper, "John Cowles Sr. blended intelligence and business acumen" and steered the paper in a more liberal direction during the Eisenhower years, which aligned with the city's long liberal history and strong union tradition, fertile ground from which sprang national Democratic leaders named Humphrey, Mondale, McCarthy, Wellstone, Ellison and others. Cowles' son, John Jr., greatly influenced Sir Tyrone Guthrie to build his regional theater here in 1963, and the paper played a major role in the development of the Metrodome. It also owned land around the proposed dome site. It officially became the *Star Tribune: Newspaper of the Twin Cities* in 1987. Many detractors at the weekly papers and its daily competitor across the river at what would become simply the *Pioneer Press* in 1990 saw the "Newspaper of the Twin Cities" tag as yet another antagonistic "Strib" assault on the "Pi Press." The phrase was later dropped.

The Ridder family, which owned other papers in the East, entered the Twin Cities market in 1927, later buying *The Duluth News Tribune*. The St. Paul paper boasts three coveted Pulitzer Prizes and a more conservative political tone. The family ownership, like the Cowles, helped both cities flourish under its practices and influence. The Ridders were "newspaper men capable, alert and of real convictions," noted the paper's preceding owner, according to a lengthy obituary-like account of *Pioneer Press* history, penned by John R. Finnegan Sr. (a former *Pioneer Press* executive editor) upon the sale of the paper in 2006 to the McClatchy Co., which ended the Ridder dynasty but not its Minnesota presence.

That character assessment was certainly true of the paper's first Ridder publisher, Ben, who was influential in attracting a pro football team and the development of the Metropolitan Opera. Ben Ridder was also tirelessly civic-minded, according to Finnegan: "By 1945, Ben admitted that he devoted only about 10 percent of his time to publishing two St. Paul dailies. He made hundreds of speeches around the state. He headed many fund drives. Once, when handed the names of six wealthy men to contact for pledges to the Community Fund and War Chest, he was turned down. He went back to the office and wrote an editorial headlined 'The Six Misers.' He did not mention any names but was blunt about their failure to make donations. The next day, 30 big contributions arrived by noon. Apparently, each donor thought he was one of the six mentioned."

Like the Strib, which Wikipedia says "scored what would turn out to be a major readership coup when it signed a deal in 1985 with Universal Press Syndicate to be the sole Minneapolis-St. Paul area carrier of a brand-new comic strip that would turn out to be one of the most influential and powerful in the history of the medium, 'Calvin and Hobbes,' " the Pi Press printed the earliest cartoons of Minnesota's native son Charles Schultz called "Li'l Folks." It later became the billion-dollar "Peanuts" franchise.

Both papers have also produced a wealth of talent and memorable columnists: At the Strib, there's the widely known CJ and fellow columnists such as Barbara Flanagan, Jim Klobucher, Sid Hartman, Pat Reusse, Nick Coleman and Dick Youngblood. Pi Press touts family expert Donna Erickson and writers including Don Boxmeyer (whose hilarious closing line was often "I'll try to miss that"), Gail MarxJarvis, Dave Beale, Larry Millett, Joe Soucheray and John Camp. Camp was one of the paper's Pulitzer Prize-winning reporters, who later left the profession to become a best-selling crime novelist under the name John Sanford (his book titles invariably feature the word Prey and are usually set in the Twin Cities).

Both papers were eventually traded on the stock market: In 1974, the Ridders combined its ownership of the *Pioneer Press* in a merger with Knight newspapers to create Knight-Ridder, also a public company. The Strib was sold to the California-based and publicly traded McClatchy Co. in 1997. In 2006, McClatchy bought Knight-Ridder's many papers, including the Pi Press, only to sell it later that same year to MediaNews Group to avoid a same-market monopoly. Then, in late-2006, the Strib was unloaded to a private investment group, Avista Capital Partners, signaling at least two rounds of buy-outs and layoffs in the newsrooms—7 percent of the company's 2,100 positions, including 50 in the news and editorial side as of May 2007.

The competition across the river had seen the same bloodletting as its ownership changed, and the same layoff scenario was happening all over the country at major city dailies. However, the sale of the *Pioneer Press* to *Star Tribune* parent company (McClatchy) brought its share of headlines related to the shocking defection of *Pioneer Press* publisher Par Ridder to the *Star Tribune*.

Both papers continue to be subject to the economic pressures of the industry and dwindling advertising dollars that keep streaming to the internet while circulation falls. Ironically, the daily papers in rural-to-mid-sized towns and cities have flourished throughout the state during much of the 1900s and continue to do so, while the larger Twin Cities dailies face new challenges. *The Mankato Free Press, Rochester Post Bulletin, St. Cloud Times, Brainerd Dispatch* and others have grown heartily.

In spring 2007, the Strib and Pi Press were engaged in a nasty legal battle over Par Ridder's move, plus the paper's recruitment of several key Pi Press personnel and the alleged theft by Ridder of a company computer with strategies, revenue figures and other operational information. "News that the 38-year-old publishing scion was leaving the Pi Press to join the long-standing rival undoubtedly had his great-grandfather doing somersaults in his grave," said Finnegan, as reported in a story about the fray in *City Pages* on April 18, 2007.

The alternative press in Minnesota has doggedly been watching and covering the mainstream press and the various subcultures, trends, underground arts and music scenes and other stories more or less since the '70s. Culturally, the weekly alternative papers in Minnesota today such as *City Pages* share a direct but rapidly fading lineage back to the era of the beats and the elementary "underground press" publications such as *The Realist*, founded in the '50s by satirist and writer Paul Krassner.

During the countercultural Flower Power era, underground weeklies sprouted in American cities like thirsty pot plants. *The Berkley Barb* (Bay area), *The Chicago Seed*, *The Rag* (Austin, Texas), et. al. eventually fueled the rich tradition of the Minneapolis-St. Paul weeklies and later the outstate rags. One of the earliest, *One Hundred Flowers*, was published by Ed Fellein, who says he got the idea for starting an underground rag after blanketing Dinkytown near the University of Minnesota with anti-Vietnam war leaflets and noticing no one was reading them.

"I thought there must be a better way to market the anti-war message, and after seeing copies of papers from other cities like *The Seed*, decided that was the way to go," Fellein said. He and a collective/commune of friends put out *Flowers* for about a year until Fellein's ardent advocacy of the Black Panther Party got him "purged" off the commune. Now he is publisher of the south Minneapolis neighborhood paper *Southside Pride* and until May 2007, the 10-year-old alternative news weekly *Pulse*, which morphed into an online daily blog format.

In the late-'70s, the Twin Cities first saw two competing interests for the weekly market: *The Twin Cities Reader* and *Metropolis*. The former—first named *The Entertainer*— was started by Mark Hopp, Deborah Hopp and a few friends in 1976 while they were working at the University of Minnesota's *Daily*. One of the nation's finest college newspapers, the *Daily* has produced a wealth of talent, among them international journalists such as Eric Sevareid, Harrison Salisbury and Harry Reasoner.

The latter paper came to the streets of Minneapolis-St. Paul like a classic carpetbagger from back East with a distinctively Ivy League pedigree and a vintage, wine-soaked name. Walter Rothchild III (nicknamed "Trip") and a couple friends he knew at Harvard and a local staff went tete-a-tete with Hopp's burgeoning weekly but gave up the fight the same year. Although *Metropolis*—purporting to be a Minnesota version of *Rolling Stone*—produced a better editorial product, it shut down in September 1977.

When the *Star Tribune* went on strike in 1980, *The Entertainer* got a break and began publishing Monday-Friday until the strike ended, with wire copy, local reporting and a heavy focus on entertainment stories, movie listings and bar ads. According to Deborah Hopp (who now is publisher of *Minneapolis-St. Paul* and other magazines), the strike readily established the paper editorially, as it began to carve a niche for itself.

Meanwhile, the downtown markets of both cities saw the rise of *Skyway News* (now *The Downtown Journal*), started by Sam Kaufman, which targeted the 9-to-5 downtown workforce. In St. Paul, *The Downtowner* attempted the same task and was the brainchild of Ron and Charlene Bacigalupo.

With *Metropolis* gone, *The Twin Cities Reader* looked like it owned its space. But in August 1979, a noisy monthly music rag imported, in part, from Portland, Maine and Boston called *Sweet Potato* hit the stands. Often called "The Spud" by its early skeleton edit and sales staff, the burgeoning paper had main monthly rivals in two struggling music papers, *NightTimes* and *Connie's Insider*. *Sweet Potato* Publisher Tom Bartel and his wife, Kristin Henning, followed the lead of one of their best friends from Carleton College, who started *Sweet Potato* back East and moved the same model to Minnesota, supplemented with stories that ran in the other Spuds. In 1980 it became a biweekly paper with other entertainment news and criticism, and eventually severed its ties to the coast. A year later it changed its name to *City Pages* and went weekly, signaling the start of one of the most embattled newspaper wars in the Twin Cities, between *City Pages* and the *Reader*.

The pressures didn't deter Mark Hopp. He acquired *Corporate Report* in '86, and started a weekly business paper called *CityBusiness* as early as 1980 (owning also *CityBusiness* New Orleans). Later, with outside investors, he purchased a string of similar business publications around the country, only to get caught up in a leveraged buyout, which put the *Reader* at risk. Hopp died in 1992 from bone marrow cancer and was posthumously inducted into the *Minnesota Daily* Hall of Distinction in 1995. The fierce battle between the *Pages* and the *Reader* came to a close in 1997 after *City Pages* was sold to Village Voice Media, which soon afterward bought the *Reader* and shut it down.

The Phoenix-based New Times Inc. eventually purchased *City Pages* in 2006, leading to the firing of a longtime columnist Jim Walsh and the testy departures of longtime staffers, Editor Steve Perry and writer Britt Robson. But with each business deal over the past 20 years—and the omniscient reaches of the internet—the weeklies seemed to lose more local color, and more cachet as alternative news sources, despite the fact that *City Pages* was the first paper in

Minnesota to write an AIDS story (1982) and landed exclusive, rare interviews with Tom Wolfe and Bob Dylan, among other distinctions. The *Reader* published an annual "Get Out of Town" issue that inflamed every public figure on it, plus heavily scrutinized the Metrodome development.

Weekly papers continue to serve both outstate and metro suburban markets. Papers like *The Hayfield Herald*, *Warroad Pioneer* and *The Hinckley Herald* provide a dish of weekly community news and advertising to smaller towns across Minnesota. But none are ultimately immune from the painful battles between newsprint and the web. In the Twin Cities alone, Minnesota Sun Publications operates 44 community papers, and the Lillie Suburban company has around a dozen, while independent papers dot communities across the state. Nonetheless, the drastic impact from diminishing classified and display ads—the lifeblood of papers big and small—is putting the industry in a serious bind. The same month of the Strib layoffs in 2007, the Sun laid off almost a dozen employees, too. As for the once ink-stained wretch who initially ignored but never forgot his boss' warning about the internet long ago in North Carolina, he's moved to the other side of the desk at a reputable public relations firm in Minneapolis. (ᴘ)

Clockwise from top left: Bernie Ridder, Sid Hartman, Deborah Hopp and Mark Hopp. Newspaper legend Bernie Ridder owned the Duluth and St. Paul dailies and part of the Vikings,
later merging his company to become Knight Ridder. Sid Hartman is one of Minnesota's
best-known media personalities. The Hopps founded the *Twin Cities Reader* and *CityBusiness*. Deb Hopp later became publisher of *Mpls St. Paul* magazine. (photos: courtesy,
Pioneer Press, Pavek Museum and *Mpls.St. Paul* magazine)

Minnesota's Daily Newspaper Towns

Albert Lea Tribune Austin Daily Herald **Bemidji Pioneer** Brainerd Dispatch **Breckenridge Daily News** Crookston Daily Times **Duluth News Tribune** Faribault Daily News **Fargo/Moorhead Forum** Fairmont Sentinal **Fergus Falls Daily Journal** Hibbing Tribune **International Falls Journal** Minneapolis Finance and Commerce **Minneapolis Star Tribune** Mankato Free Press **Marshall Independent** New Ulm Journal **Owatonna People's Press** Red Wing Republican Eagle **Rochester Post Bulletin** St. Cloud Times **St. Paul Pioneer Press** Stillwater Gazette **Mesabi Daily News** West Central Tribune **Winona Daily News** Worthington Daily Globe

These newspaper titles became the *Pioneer Press*, *The Business Journal* and *Star Tribune*.

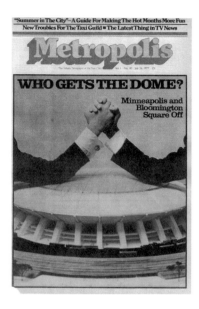

Metropolis, The Entertainer, The Twin Cities Reader and *Sweet Potato* were all forerunners to today's modern alternative weeklies. Covers from the '70s and '80s show how things have changed, or did they?

Hamms Beer and The Hamms Bear became advertising icons through the work of Campbell-Mithun in Minneapolis. (graphic: courtesy Campbell-Mithun)

Advertising
From the Land of Sky Blue Water

I t all comes back to the water. Minnesota's advertising industry is intricately linked to the state's heritage as a flour milling giant, fueled by the storied Mississippi River.

Powered by St. Anthony Falls, flour mills began flourishing in Minneapolis in the mid-1850s, supplied with wheat grown by new settlers in Minnesota and the Dakotas. Between 1880 and 1930, Minneapolis led the nation in flour production, earning it the nickname "Mill City."

Cadwallader C. Washburn's Minneapolis mill, built in 1866, was touted as the largest mill west of Buffalo, N.Y. By the early-1900s, three Minneapolis corporations controlled 97 percent of the nation's flour production: Washburn-Crosby Co. (which became General Mills); Pillsbury-Washburn Flour Mills Co. (which became Pillsbury Flour Mills Co.); and Northwestern Consolidated Milling Co. (which became the Standard Milling Co.). This Minneapolis "Flour Trust" dominated the national flour market until the 1930s and provided the basis for early commerce in Minneapolis.

Meanwhile, we grew. In 1902, George Dayton opened his dry goods store in a new Minneapolis building; in ensuing years, the store would provide much advertising activity in Minnesota and the country (becoming, by the late-1990s, the fourth-largest retailer in the United States). In 1912, Minneapolis businesses joined forces, amassed a fund of $3,000 and launched the forerunner of the national

Better Business Bureau, as Minneapolis Advertising Forum's "Vigilance Committee." By 1914, the Vigilance Committee hired a full-time manager to review advertising and ensure that truthful advertising took place.

But looking back, it seems there would be little to be vigilant about in those infancy days of Minnesota advertising, when innocent cartoon characters popped up as product spokespeople, who would live on in our collective memories, fondly recalled, for a lifetime. In fact, *Ad Age* magazine named three advertising characters introduced by Minnesota companies—The Green Giant, Betty Crocker and the Pillsbury doughboy—among the top 10 top advertising icons of the 20th century.

Flour mills began marketing their products. Washburn-Crosby branded its flour "Gold Medal" in recognition of a prize won in 1880, and advertised with the slogan "Eventually—Why Not Now?" Pillsbury launched its slogan, "Because Pillsbury's Best," incorporating their brand name "Pillsbury's Best."

In 1921, Washburn-Crosby created one of advertising's most enduring symbols when it introduced Betty Crocker. According to the article "Betty Crocker: Marketing the Modern Woman" in the spring 1999 issue of *Hennepin History*: "Behind the creative genius of Betty Crocker were many talented individuals employed by Washburn-Crosby. One in particular, Samuel Gale, is credited as the driving force behind Betty. … He understood from the hundreds of letters the company received each week that the modern age of homemaking had left many ill-prepared for their responsibilities. He took it upon himself and his small staff to reply to each letter personally, but he never felt right about signing his own name."

After a promotion for Gold Medal flour offered consumers a pin cushion resembling a flour sack if they correctly completed a jigsaw puzzle of a milling scene, Washburn-Crosby was panicked by the 30,000 responses to the contest as well as the flood of questions about baking. Spurred by Gale and the contest response, the company invented a friendly female figurehead whose name would be used on correspondence. "Crocker" was chosen to honor a recently retired director of the company. "Betty" was just Minnesota nice-sounding. Female employees were invited to submit sample Betty Crocker signatures; the one judged most distinctive is the basis for the one still used today.

Long before Martha touted good things, Betty Crocker was the first female multimedia superstar. Washburn-Crosby purchased a Minneapolis radio station in 1924 and renamed it WCCO, standing for "Washburn Crosby Company." Beginning in 1924, Betty hosted the country's first radio cooking show, *Betty Crocker School of the Air,* first in the Twin Cities and later on the NBC radio network. In 1945, she would be voted second most-famous woman in America after Eleanor Roosevelt, according to *Fortune.* Later still, she would have her own television show, which would run for 22 years.

In the 1920s, the Odell family of Minnesota began making Burma-Shave shaving cream, and advertising the product on folksy roadside signs. Each sign had one line about the product, and usually about four signs placed along the road in succession made up the entire message. The first signs, along Highway 35 in Minnesota in 1925, were a success, leading to expansion into neighboring states. As the signs appeared alongside more highways across the nation, they became embedded in the American roadside culture. To optimize advertising space, often the signs featured slogans on both sides to catch the attention of travelers going in opposite directions.

> *IF YOU DON'T KNOW*
> *WHOSE SIGNS THESE ARE*
> *YOU CAN'T HAVE DRIVEN*
> *VERY FAR*
> —*Burma-Shave*

Burma-Shave invited customers to invent jingles for their signs, awarding $100 for winning entries. Throughout the nearly 40-year campaign, there were at least 600 slogans on more than 7,000 sets of signs. The signs appeared in all but four of the contiguous states. But eventually, superhighways and supersized billboards were the campaign's demise, and by the mid-1960s, Burma-Shave's sign campaign was history.

In 1924, Wheaties was born after someone accidentally spilled wheat bran on a hot stove, creating wheat flakes. The result was brought to the attention of the head miller at the Washburn Crosby Co., George Cormack, who perfected the process of producing the ready-to-eat cereal (named "Wheaties" by an employee's wife, who won the product-naming contest). In 1926, Wheaties broke new ground when the world's first singing commercial was performed on Christmas Eve by four male singers. The Wheaties Quartet (consisting of an undertaker, a bailiff, a printer and a businessman) would sing that song over the air for the next six years at $6 per singer per week. By 1929, General Mills was ready to drop the Wheaties brand. But General Mills' advertising manager, Sam Gale (the same Sam who concocted Betty Crocker), pointed out that the 23,000 of the 53,0000 cases sold nationwide had been sold in Minneapolis-St. Paul, where the singing commercials had aired. Soon the ads aired nationwide, and Wheaties sales climbed steadily. In 1932, CBS bought WCCO and kept the acronym WCCO as call letters.

Wheaties ventured into sports marketing in 1933 via a sign on the leftfield wall at old Nicollet Park in south Minneapolis. General Mills' broadcast deal with the minor league Minneapolis Millers on WCCO included the large signboard that Wheaties used to introduce its new advertising slogan. The late Knox Reeves (of the Minneapolis-based advertising agency that bore his name) was asked what should be printed on the signboard for his client. He sketched a Wheaties package, and then printed: "Wheaties—The Breakfast of Champions." So the story goes. From that modest beginning, Wheaties went on to honor the greatest athletes of all time. The brand also played a role in king-making: After Wheaties began sponsoring baseball radio broadcasts, Ronald "Dutch" Reagan was voted the country's most popular Wheaties baseball announcer in 1937, which earned him a free trip to California, where he did screen tests. He never returned!)

In 1928, Minnesota Valley Canning (founded in 1903 in LeSueur) introduced an icon to promote its new vegetable

brand. But according to *Ad Age*, "The Green Giant's national
ad debut in 1928 was disappointing. ... in his earliest days he
was stooped and scowling, wore a scruffy bearskin and looked
more like the Incredible Hulk than the grand old gardener he
is today. ... The assignment for the Giant's transformation was
tackled by none other than young Leo Burnett, who improved
the Giant's hunched posture, turned his scary scowl into a
sunny smile and clothed him in a light, leafy outfit. ..." By
1950, Minnesota Valley changed its name to Green Giant Co.

In 1926, an advertising character by the name of Reddy
Kilowatt made his way to Minnesota as corporate spokesman
for electricity. Reddy—a stick figure whose body and limbs
are made of "lightning bolt" symbols and whose head has a
light bulb for a nose and sockets for ears—was created by the
Alabama Power Co. and licensed by 200 electrical companies.
In 1998, Reddy was bought by Minnesota-based Northern
States Power Co. (now Xcel Energy).

Campbell-Mithun Advertising opened its doors during
the Great Depression, in 1933, in downtown Minneapolis—its
two principals hailing from BBDO's Minneapolis office.
That year, Pres. Franklin D. Roosevelt issued a nationwide
Bank Holiday, closing all banks to prevent further panic, and
Campbell-Mithun began life in the vacated offices of a failed
bank with a staff of five.

The first three accounts of Campbell-Mithun were
Andersen Corp., Land O'Lakes and Northwestern National
Bank. Land O'Lakes' Indian maiden icon was created during a
search for a brand name and trademark. In 1939, the brand's
image was refined by illustrator Jess Betlach. (In 1959, another

Minneapolis company would also launch its brand with an Indian maiden image. Minneapolis Gas Co. first used the name of Minnegasco and an Indian maiden cartoon figure that year. The company is now Center Point Energy.)

Knox Reeves opened his Minneapolis agency in the early-'30s. Other advertising agencies and related businesses began to spring up. In 1938, an industrious, young Curtis Carlson launched his Gold Bond Stamp Co. in the Plymouth Building in downtown Minneapolis. After years of struggle, he eventually landed the SuperValu Food Store chain, and the Carlson empire flourished. Martin/Williams Inc. started in 1947, with Creamettes pasta products as a major account.

In 1948 KSTP signed on in the Twin Cities as the only television station west of Chicago and the first NBC affiliate in the nation. Just in time for Hamm's:

In 1952, Campbell-Mithun introduced Hamm's Beer. The original jingle was derived from "From the Land of Sky-Blue Water," a 1909 song with lyrics by Nelle Richmond Eberhart and music by Charles Wakefield Cadman. It started with the beating of tom-tom drums, after which a chorus intoned:

> *From the Land of Sky Blue Waters,*
> *From the land of pines, lofty balsams,*
> *Comes the beer refreshing,*
> *Hamm's the beer refreshing.*

The first television commercial depicted animated beavers beating their tails to the tom-tom beat of the jingle, as well as live action shots of the forests and lakes. The second, produced in 1952, introduced the dancing black-and-white cartoon beer bear named "Sascha," which proved so popular it was used for the next three decades.

According to beer historian Carl H. Miller, in his 2002 article, "Beer and Television: Perfectly Tuned In": "Never were the advantages of animation better exploited than in the long-running commercials featuring the wacky-go-lucky Hamm's bear. ... In 1965, the Audit Research Bureau reported that the bear ranked first in 'best liked' advertisements nationwide, an impressive achievement considering that Hamm's commercials aired in only 31 states.

"At least two aspects of the Hamm's bear commercials were critical to their overwhelming success. First, each spot was, in itself, a miniature story, complete with plot, characters, conflict and (if the bear was lucky) resolution. The spots had genuine entertainment value and elicited good viewer attention. Second, the animation and interspersed real-life shots dramatically showcased Minnesota's pristine wilderness ... in order to drive home the Hamm's theme: 'From the Land of Sky Blue Waters.' "

Carmichael Lynch entered the Minnesota advertising scene in 1962. Colorful cofounder Lee Lynch recalls that the first few years were so rough that he took a job as a teacher at a school for delinquent girls to earn a little extra money. "I never told anybody," he told *Minneapolis/St. Paul Business Journal* in 2005. "I always faked a client engagement." Later lauded for its recreation-related ads, the Minneapolis-based shop grew to become one of the largest independently owned agencies in the nation before it was sold.

Adding to the hometown advertising activity: In 1963, Best Buy got its start as Sound of Music. Two years later, giggling his way to spokescharacter superstardom, Poppin' Fresh, the Pillsbury Doughboy, introduced himself to TV viewers across the nation in 1965, created by Leo Burnett in Chicago.

In the 1960s and '70s Knox Reeves created unique outdoor boards for Grain Belt Beer and Minnegasco. Campbell-Mithun launched a series of award-winning commercials for Northwest Orient Airlines. Colle+McVoy turned second-string Minnesota Viking lineman Bob Lurtsema into a cult hero for Twin City Federal. BBDO made memorable ads for Austin-based Hormel.

Twin Cities TV personality Mel Jass became the best-known television pitchman in Minnesota. Jass, known for his live commercials on Channel 11's *Matinee Movie*, had the knack of doing commercials live, without rehearsals or cue cards. Soon, from Duluth to Rochester, advertisers created pitchmen and women to hawk their wares: Rudy, Ken and Jerry Boschwitz (Plywood Minnesota), the Tousley Ford guy, Jack Prescott, bankruptcy attorney ("This is all I do and I do it well"), the Goldfines (for their Duluth department store), George Corporaal (giving away boxes of steaks for Glass Service Company), Hal Greenwood (Midwest Federal), Nancy Nelson, Dick Enrico, Denny Hecker, The Menards Guy, Geno Palucci, Mama Vitale, Rose Totino, Bill Diehl, Timothy D. Kehr.

The Minnesota ad industry started making waves nationally in the early-1980s. It was no longer "flyover land." Fallon McElligott and Rice (now Fallon World Wide) launched in 1981 and soon put Minnesota advertising on the map with print ads featuring bold headlines. An ad for the Episcopal Church asked, "Whose birthday is it anyway?" above pictures of Jesus Christ and Santa Claus. Fallon's trade campaign for *Rolling Stone* magazine titled "Perception/Reality" juxtaposed images of the magazine's perceived audience: hippies in Earth shoes with psychedelic-painted Volkswagen buses, against its actual readership—yuppies in Nikes with Ford Mustangs. The agency won highly visible national accounts and was named Agency of the Year.

By the late-'90s, the glory days had come to advertising, and Minnesota flourished. Mergers and acquisitions swept the advertising industry. New media came into the mainstream, paving the way for new interative agencies like Risdall Linnihan, and the landscape changed for clients and agencies locally.

In the new century in the Mill City, the economy forced agencies to do more with less. General Mills acquired its rival Pillsbury in 2001. Campbell-Mithun, Fallon, Martin/Williams, Carmichael Lynch, Colle+McVoy, Kerker and Periscope are the big names in advertising in town. Lee Lynch announced his retirement from Carmichael Lynch in 2005. In 2006, the Advertising Federation of Minnesota celebrated 100 years. Time marches on.

Through it all, Minnesota has embraced its advertising heritage. Burma Shave was re-introduced in 1997. In 2000, the *St. Paul Pioneer Press* named the Hamm's bear a runner-up on its list of "150 Influential Minnesotans of the Past 150 Years." And somewhere in our kitchen cupboards, there's a picture of Betty or an Indian maiden to bring it all back home. ((¡))

Ray Mithun, the Godfather of Minnesota advertising, started Campbell-Mithun in the 1930s. The agency has grown to one of the country's largest.
(photo: courtesy Campbell-Mithun)

Pat Fallon, whose agency put Minneapolis on the creative map, has worked with *Rolling Stone* magazine and BMW among other large national and international clients. Fallon also co-authored the book *Juicing the Orange*. (photo: courtesy Fallon Worldwide)

Betty Crocker, a native Minnesotan, has evolved over the years as an enduring symbol for General Mills.

Bob Lurtsema of the Vikings was long featured in ads for TCF by Colle McVoy Advertising.

While acting at Excelsior's Old Log Theater in the 1970s, Nick Nolte is remembered as the T-shirted spokesman for NSP. In a series of ads and with a squint, Nolte encouraged Minnesotans to "use energy wisely." Nolte went on to energize Hollywood within years after these commercials aired. (photo: Old Log Theater)

Left, Lee Lynch, on the cover of Minnesota's *Format* magazine, used wit and wisdom to grow Carmichael Lynch into a national advertising powerhouse whose clients have included Harley Davidson and The Minnesota Lottery. John Risdall, who founded his ad agency in the '70s has parlayed marketing and creative savvy into national success. (photo: courtesy RAA)

Minnesota-based Gold'n Plump Poultry's Chicken has entertained millions nationally in ads originally created by Fallon McElligott Rice. (image: courtesy Gold'n Plump Poultry)

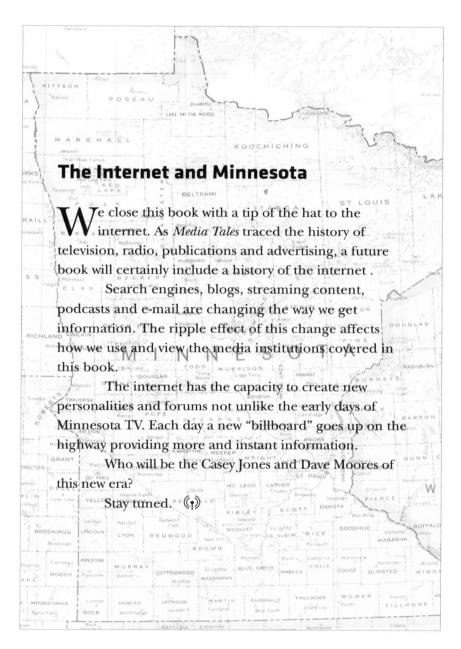

The Internet and Minnesota

We close this book with a tip of the hat to the internet. As *Media Tales* traced the history of television, radio, publications and advertising, a future book will certainly include a history of the internet .

Search engines, blogs, streaming content, podcasts and e-mail are changing the way we get information. The ripple effect of this change affects how we use and view the media institutions covered in this book.

The internet has the capacity to create new personalities and forums not unlike the early days of Minnesota TV. Each day a new "billboard" goes up on the highway providing more and instant information.

Who will be the Casey Jones and Dave Moores of this new era?

Stay tuned.

About the Authors

Sheri O'Meara

Sheri O'Meara is editor of The Minnesota Series, co-author of the first book in the series, *Storms!*, and will be author of the next book, *Storms 2*. She is also currently editor of *Minnesota Meetings and Events* magazine and has served as founding editor of monthly publications for K102-FM (where she was recognized by *Billboard* magazine for her work on *Minnesota Country* magazine), Sun Country Airlines and SimonDelivers. As editor of *Format Magazine*, she covered Minnesota's advertising and media industries for 10 years, the magazine receiving a Crystal Clarion Award from Minnesota Women in Communications. She has managed magazines for organizations including The Guthrie Theater and Minnesota Orchestra, and has written for a variety of Twin Cities publications. Sheri is also lead singer in the Twin Cities-based Celtic band Locklin Road. She has performed in Ireland at international songwriter showcase concerts and locally at venues including Minnesota State Fair and Minnesota Irish Fair.

Martin Keller

Martin Keller is author of *Music Legends* and co-author of *Storms!*, the first two books in the Minnesota Series. He has worked as a journalist, screenplay writer, pop culture critic and public relations professional over the past 30 years. His work has appeared nationally in *Leaders*, *Rolling Stone*, *Billboard*, *The Washington Post*, *The Boston Globe*, *Final Frontier*, *Utne Reader* and locally in *The Journal of Law & Politics*, *Corporate Report*, *CityBusiness*, *Minnesota Monthly*, *The Star Tribune*, *The Pioneer Press*, *City Pages* and *Twin Cities Reader*. He has appeared on *Today Show*, *48 Hours*, public television and Minnesota Public Radio. Awards include a Minnesota Film Fund Award from the McKnight Foundation and Blockbuster Video and an International Association of Business Communicators Award for Excellence. Keller has also co-written four screenplays and developed two television pilots. He practices public relations with his own company, Media Savant Communications Co.

ACCESS MINNESOTA

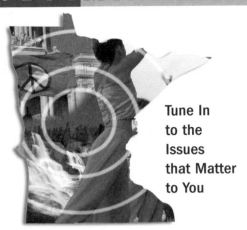

Tune In
to the
Issues
that Matter
to You

Each week, **Access Minnesota** brings you University of Minnesota faculty experts, the state's political leaders and other notable newsmakers for an in-depth look at timely issues. From the State Legislature to Iraq to the environment to popular culture, Access Minnesota keeps you well informed. **Access Minnesota ... Issues that Matter to You.**

Access Minnesota is produced in collaboration with:

Heard on these stations:

KIKV	100.7	FM	Alexandria	KKOJ	1190	AM	Jackson	KLCI	106.1	FM	Princeton
KXRA	1490	AM	Alexandria	KDOG	96.7	FM	Mankato	WQPM	1300	AM	Princeton
KBMO	1290	AM	Benson	KRRW	101.5	FM	Mankato	KLGR	1490	AM	Redwood Falls
KSCR	93.5	FM	Benson	KXAC	100.5	FM	Mankato	KOLM	1520	AM	Rochester
KLKS	104.3	FM	Breezy Point	KDWB	101.3	FM	Minneapolis	KROC	1340	AM	Rochester
KSMM	1530	AM	Chaska	KEEY	102.1	FM	Minneapolis	KNSI	1450	AM	St. Cloud
KROX	1260	AM	Crookston	KFAN	1130	AM	Minneapolis	KVSC	88.1	FM	St. Cloud
KDLM	1340	AM	Detroit Lakes	KMNV	1400	AM	Minneapolis	WDGY	630	AM	St. Paul
KDAL	610	AM	Duluth	KQQL	107.9	FM	Minneapolis	WMIN	740	AM	St. Paul
KRBR	102.5	FM	Duluth	KTCZ	97.1	FM	Minneapolis	KLBB	1220	AM	Stillwater
KTCO	98.9	FM	Duluth	KTLK	100.3	FM	Minneapolis	KSRQ	90.1	FM	Thief River Falls
WDSM	710	AM	Duluth	KTNF	950	AM	Minneapolis	KTRF	1230	AM	Thief River Falls
WGEE	970	AM	Duluth	KUOM	770	AM	Minneapolis	KKWQ	92.5	FM	Warroad
KMFY	96.9	FM	Grand Rapids	KXFN	690	AM	Minneapolis	KWLM	1340	AM	Willmar
KOZY	1320	AM	Grand Rapids	KUMM	89.7	FM	Morris	KKLN	94.1	FM	Willmar
WNMT	650	AM	Hibbing	KJOE	106.1	FM	Pipestone	KWOA	730	AM	Worthington
KARP	1260	AM	Hutchinson	KLOH	1050	AM	Pipestone				

**www.accessminnesotaonline.com
for broadcast times**

Coming Up

Storm Clouds Ahead!

We kicked off The Minnesota Series with *Storms!* Now, hold onto your Dopplers ... *Storms 2* comes rolling in with:

The 1930s Dust Bowl, Minnesota's top weather event of the 20th century.

The worst tornadoes in Twin Cities history, striking in May 1965.

The Edina/Roseville Tornadoes of 1981.

The Red River Valley Flooding of 1997 ... and much more.

Don't miss this great gift book, coming up next in The Minnesota Series!

Also watch for:

Political Stars

From famous families—(the Mondales, Humphreys and Colemans) to the "Rudys" (Perpich and Boschwitz) to Minnesota's first congresswoman (Coya Knutson) to our most colorful governor ever (Jesse Ventura)—Minnesota politicians make for the most remarkable stories.

Don't miss these engaging tales as well as the inside stories of Eugene McCarthy, Paul Wellstone, Al Franken and others!